LOUIS SULLIVAN
An Architect in American Thought

Sherman Paul

LOUIS
SULLIVAN

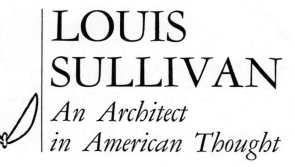

An Architect
in American Thought

A SPECTRUM BOOK

PRENTICE-HALL, INC. · ENGLEWOOD CLIFFS, N. J.

For Lewis and Sophia Mumford

CONTENTS

PREFACE

Louis Sullivan was born in New England in the time of Emerson, Thoreau, and Whitman. He died in Chicago in 1924, when a new generation animated in its own way by the earlier transcendental impulse was achieving a new expression. More than any other artist of his generation he assimilated and united the organic philosophy and democratic aspiration of the earlier time and in his own building and writing transmitted them to a new generation. He spans the generations, having found for the transcendental vision new warrants in the thought of men like Dewey, Veblen, and William James. In his work we witness both continuity and transformation: the idealism of transcendentalism—its reassessment of the creative power of man—is naturalized in an equally idealistic pragmatism; what is properly individual, man's creative impulse, is broadened in its aims, from self-culture to social-culture; *laissez faire* individualism, disciplined by an education in choice and responsibility, is socialized; and the environmental benefits of rural life, insisted on but not sentimentalized, are brought forward as possibilities of a more vital urban culture. As Lewis Mumford was the first to realize, "Sullivan's was perhaps the first mind in American architecture that had come to know itself with any fullness in relation to its soil, its period, its civilization, and had been able to absorb fully the many lessons of the century."

Mumford was also right in calling Sullivan "the Whitman of American architecture." No architect—indeed, no writer—took more from Whitman or taught so fervently his gospel of democracy. Sullivan believed in the moral influence of architecture, which Whitman said had "capacities, and a real future. . . ." He spent his life both as an architect and writer in trying to bring America to "form" and in trying to express what Whitman hoped America would express, the "deepest basic elements and loftiest final meanings, of history and man. . . ." Always addressing his major work to the "laity," he wrote much that both implements Whitman's gospel and synthesizes the new thought of his time. If one remembers that in Sullivan's day sociology was the new master science, then his work, which includes studies in psychology, pedagogy, history, and philosophy, might be appropriately called a sociology of democracy. No American architect has written so cogently or so well, compelling attention as a thinker and literary artist; none has a better claim to a permanent place in our intellectual history. To place Sullivan in our intellectual tradition is the purpose of this essay.

I have benefitted of course from much that has been written about Sullivan-the-architect. To master another discipline is the work of many years and in architecture, where buildings must be known and experienced in the way one knows and experiences a poem, a work of arduous devotion. I have seen many of Sullivan's buildings but have not lived with them; I have looked frequently at photographs and found none more admirable or sympathetic than those of John Szarkowski (*The Idea of Louis Sullivan*). An increase in knowledge and familiarity however is not necessarily an increase in competence. Certainly in matters of architecture and even in matters of intellectual history, where I am heartened by the excellent work on Sullivan by Richard P. Adams, Donald Drew Egbert, Ray Ginger, Paul Goodman, and Elaine Hedges, I acknowledge the suitability of Ibn Khaldun's remark: "The capital of knowledge that an individual scholar has to offer is small. Admission of one's shortcomings saves from censure. Kindness from colleagues is hoped for."

I have many debts: to Ruth E. Schoneman, librarian of the Ryerson and Burnham Libraries of the Art Institute of Chicago, and to Adolf K. Placzek of The Avery Library of Columbia University for the use of Sullivan's manuscripts; to Cerilla Saylor, librarian of The Ricker Library of Architecture, and Eva F. Benton, librarian of the English Library, at the University of Illinois for generous interest and assistance; to the Research Board of the University of Illinois for funds and to the Center for Advanced Study of the University of Illinois which granted me an associate membership, for the time needed to complete this work; to Geraldine Bogart, my research assistant, for bibliographical help; to Richard Nickel for permitting me to read his master's paper on Sullivan's ornament and for his generous use of photographs; to Elaine Hedges for permitting me to read the proof of her introduction to *Democracy: A Man-Search*; to Jack Stillinger, Robert Schneider, Dwight Miller, Walter Creese, Allen Weller, and Allen Brooks for their willingness in listening and their stimulating response to my ideas; to Robert Schneider and Robert McColley for carefully reading the text; and to my wife who heard it all day by day and who, with those to whom this book is dedicated, contributed most.

S. P.
Urbana, Illinois

*Beauty will not come at the call of a legislature,
nor will it repeat in England or America its history
in Greece. It will come, as always, unannounced,
and spring up between the feet of brave and earnest
men.*

> *Ralph Waldo Emerson, cited on the title page
> of Mrs.* Schuyler Van Rensselaer's Henry
> Hobson Richardson and His Works (1888),
> *a volume in Sullivan's library.*

THE ARCHITECT WHO IS HE AND WHY

*He is a relentless observer. He is always active
and effective in the investigation of Nature.*

*He sees that all forms of Nature are interde-
pendent and arise out of each other, according to
the laws of Creation.*

*In his every design a bit of Nature enters into
building.*

*His perceptions (insight) science later verifies.
Intimacy with Nature is the great friendship.
He sees ideas as also manifest actions of Nature.
It is the poet in him that is the great quality
in him.*

*The profound naturalness of his own being is
the essential condition of a great architect and a
condition of greatness in the man.*

*Expect of him a system of philosophy and ethics
which is a synthesis of society and civilization.*

> *Frank Lloyd Wright on Sullivan in* Genius
> and the Mobocracy.

1: STARTING FROM PAUMANOK

 Strasburg cathedral is a material counterpart of the soul of Erwin of Steinbach.
Ralph Waldo Emerson, *"History"* (1841)

The Autobiography of an Idea, with which Louis Sullivan concluded his life's work, is among other things a record of growth by means of rejection and acceptance. It is an *education,* like Henry Adams', that assesses the conditions of nurture. Sullivan's greatest acceptance, however, the most sustaining nutriment of his life, was acknowledged by him earlier, and elsewhere:

> CHICAGO, *Feb. 3rd, 1887.*
> *My dear and honored Walt Whitman:*
> *It is less than a year ago that I made your acquaintance so to speak, quite by accident, searching among the shelves of a book store. I was attracted by the curious title: Leaves of Grass, opened the book at random, and my eyes met the lines of Elemental Drifts. You then and there entered my soul, have not departed, and never will depart.*
> *Be assured that there is at least one (and I hope there*

are many others) who understand you as you wish to be understood; one, moreover, who has weighed you in the balance of his intuition and finds you the greatest of poets.

To a man who can resolve himself into subtle unison with Nature and Humanity as you have done, who can blend the soul harmoniously with materials, who sees good in all and overflows in sympathy toward all things, enfolding them with his spirit: to such a man I joyfully give the name of Poet—the most precious of all names.

At the time I first met your work, I was engaged upon the essay which I herewith send you. ["Inspiration," a prose poem read before the third annual convention of the Western Association of Architects, Chicago, November 17, 1886.] *I had just finished Decadence. In the Spring Song and the Song of the Depths my orbit responded to the new attracting sun. I send you this essay because it is your opinion above all other opinions that I should most highly value. What you may say in praise or encouragement will please me, but sympathetic surgery will better please. I know that I am not presuming, for have you not said: "I concentrate toward them that are nigh"—"will you speak before I am gone? Will you prove already too late?"*

After all, words fail me in writing to you. Imagine that I have expressed to you my sincere conviction of what I owe you.

The essay is my first effort, at the age of thirty. I, too, "have sweated through fog with linguists and contenders." I, too, "have pried through the strata, analyzed to a hair," reaching for the basis of a virile and indigenous art. Holding on in silence to this day, for fear of foolish utterances, I hope at least that my words may carry the weight of conviction.

Trusting that it may not be in vain that I hope to hear from you, believe me, noble man, affectionately your distant friend,

Louis H. Sullivan

Whitman relished this letter;[1] it may have reminded him of his own eloquent testimonial to Emerson and of the long foreground of his work—the simmering that Emerson brought to a boil. For Sullivan, then engaged in work on his largest commission, the Auditorium Building, the letter represents a crisis in the ferment of thought: it marks his beginning as architect and writer.

Sullivan found in Whitman the preëminent teacher and creative personality. Moses Woolson and John Edelmann disciplined and extended his youthful powers; Wagner and Michelangelo overwhelmed him with the personal force of their creations. But no one else stirred so deeply the heart of inspiration within him or provided him at the proper moment with a democratic program for thought and action.

Sullivan's debt to Whitman was so apparent, so much of the grain of his own work, that there was perhaps no need for the author of the *Autobiography* to rehearse it. Everything he wrote from the time of "Inspiration," and much that he built, is an elaboration and enrichment of Whitman's gospel, transmitted with renewed vitality in the utterance of word and stone. Thus, at the close of his life, when he told the story of his quest, Sullivan *had become* the child who went forth every day and who, in manhood, had widened the democratic vista.

The *Autobiography* begs many biographical questions. Sullivan had at hand some personal and family records, but he used these sparingly, and more often suppressed them. He did not mention his older brother, Albert, who had shared so much of his early life and who, as a railroad executive, had achieved an American success. The narrative of his own success ends with Darkmar Adler taking the younger designer into partnership. He does not tell how he developed the mature philosophy of "Face to Face," or how, in the battle for that philosophy, he was possessed by the apocalyptic vision of democracy and architecture with which the book ends.

The unmentioned years were years of "failure"—perhaps reason enough for a proud man to omit them. But his decision to emphasize the story of his childhood, boyhood, adolescence, and young manhood was also determined by his idea that the child is "the unsullied well-spring of power." [2] He believed with Thoreau that every child begins the world anew, and with the psychologist A. F. Chamberlain that the child is the "evolutionary being of our species, he in whom the useless past tends to be suppressed and the beneficial future to be foretold." [3] He learned from Taine that genius and talent were normal endowments—"gifts like seeds." [4] The child needed only a favorable soil and loving gardeners. And he had absorbed a whole philosophy of growth from Whitman's "There Was a Child Went Forth." "Is not the child the artist?" he had asked in an early address to architects. "If others were so much to him, and so influenced him, if all the objects he looked upon and received with wonder, pity, love, or dread, so wrought upon him that in sympathy he became them, and that, absorbing them they became a part of him, will not they, when he, so enriched, seeks to voice himself, will not they indeed live again and show again in that work which he must perforce of his very nature regard with such warmth of love that it becomes himself and he it?" [5]

Why tell more, if, as it turned out when the writing led him into the depths of memory, he could clearly point to those gardeners who had cared for him and to those objects that in wonder, pity, love, and dread he had become? Of these profound experiences, the *Autobiography* speaks convincingly. Its clues and indirections (against the factual background of

Willard Connely's popular biography)[6] tell the essential story of Sullivan's early years.

Louis Henri Sullivan was born in Boston on September 3, 1856. The *Autobiography* does not begin with this event—Sullivan remarks later that "he was born of woman in the usual way . . ."—but with what may have been his first cherished memory and, since the child is a seed, the most important fact of his life: his arrival, as a boy of five, at his Grandfather List's farm in South Reading. Here he had found both favoring nature and love. Here, if not in Boston where he was "Irish," he had in setting and experience an American origin. South Reading "was a main street of the day and generation," he notes, "and so was the farm proper to its time and place." The child who went forth identified with pre-Civil War rural America. His life was to be polarized between the country and the city, the environmental antagonists of the future. Even as an architect of hotels, department stores, and skyscrapers, he remained deeply loyal to the pastoral America of Emerson and Whitman.

His origins were "mongrel." He could not claim, as Mrs. Schuyler Van Rennselaer had for Richardson, a Dr. Priestley in the family. To say that "the stock was sound" was not a concession to fashionable (and racist) notions of good heredity; it was rather the sport and humor of a debunker. His father, Patrick Sullivan, was an "unlovely" Irishman with "small repulsive eyes—the eyes of a pig." Abandoned at a fair, he had climbed unaided out of poverty, come to America in 1847, and established a successful dancing academy in Boston. "He always was successful," the son comments, hinting at feelings more ambiguous than those of a father-worshiping Benjamin Franklin. Except for his romantic love of nature and his love of dance—of grace, rhythm, and symmetry which were "humanizing and beneficial"—he was without sentiment. The son found him grim, indifferent, and incapable of love; he suggests that Patrick Sullivan married Andrienne List in 1852 "as a business asset." The dancing master was too busy for many of the offices of paternity but he practiced that of disciplinarian; never permissive, he was nevertheless, in the reckoning of a son still eager to love, a wise teacher, his only successful teacher until the age of eight.

His mother, seventeen years younger than her husband, figures frequently in the *Autobiography* as the "greatly beloved mother of Louis Sullivan." The lineage of this emotional girl, gifted in music and drawing, was French, German, Swiss—and possibly Italian. She came to Boston in 1850, with her parents, Henri and Anna Mattheus List. Having failed in business in Geneva, the Lists chose "to forget the past and start anew in a strange land." They acquired a twenty-four acre farm north of Boston.

Henri List was neither farmer nor business man. Born in Hanover, he had studied theology at Göttingen and Berlin. A lectureship at the University had brought him to Geneva. There he abandoned scholarship for business—for Anna Mattheus' linen shop. The passion of this genial skeptic, who emerges as a kind of village atheist, was astronomy; the grandeur and mystery of the stars were his religion. This religion of nature fortunately included the sublunar activities of the grandson; it made him careful and permissive with the child. His wife, considerably older and more conventional, was a *mère de famille*. She looked after the family economies and respectabilities. She tutored in French to supplement the family income, but she rode to the Baptist Church in a carriage. Neither Andrienne nor Patrick was religious; Patrick found a thinker and orator in Theodore Parker. And she saw to it—at least in the beginning—that her grandson, properly dressed in pantalettes, attended the village church and school. She was not domineering, however, but simple and kind; her affection was "all-embracing." The supreme tribute of the grandson was to depict her as a Whitmanian mother.

The Lists did not immediately provide a "nest" for the boy. His earliest years were spent in the city, where he absorbed the rhythms of street cleaning, the "songs" of work and action outside his window. Describing his growth as a "breaking in from the outside and [a] breaking out from the inside," he recalled some formative incidents—and their psychic equivalents: at three, his mother's piano playing had made him sob, had opened the flood gates of feeling; later, having been rescued from a well, he had discovered when standing before the fire his "nakedness"; and watching his father at sea in a boat, he had sensed the strife and power in the world. There was little else to recall. Primary school left no memories; like much of his history of schools, it was a history of "prison." Primary school had "dulled his faculties, slackened his frank eagerness, ignored his abundant imagination, his native sympathy." That perhaps explains why the child had to await the release of the farm to go forth.

Villages seldom afford good education, and the one-room school at South Reading did little for the independent boy. The outdoors offered more and made him a truant to meaningless discipline, much to the amusement of his grandfather, who wisely gave him a garden of his own. In his first winter out-of-doors, he watched the ice-cutters and was thrilled by the booming of the ice. As thaws and rivulets heralded spring, he discovered the seasons he had taken for granted and responded to the mystery of earth—that moving, joy-bringing drama of renewal which he speaks of as the song of growth. This experience of the "joy of living" ill-prepared him for the hell-fire preaching he heard in church. He felt that the world of the preacher was "all upside down, all distorted, cruel and sugary," and he rejected it, ever afterwards to juxtapose the joy of nature to the fear engendered by religion. He did not heed this religion: by going forth into nature he was creating his own.

The first object that he became was a gigantic, solitary ash tree. This overwhelming tree on the crest of a hill was "*his* tree —his Great Friend," protective and paternal.[7] It soon shared his affection with another tree of incomparable beauty, a magnificent elm that he personified as "she." Encouraged by his grandfather to watch the world awaken, he became the sunrise too. He spent the days of his truancy educating himself at the pond and in the garden, where he felt the flowers grow; he wandered to the village to watch the workers and craftsmen— "his mighty men"; and he listened to the Irish hired girl's fairy tales. He established a pleasant domain of his own in a meadow and a marsh bordered by gloomy pines which "he contemplated for a while, and saw that all thus far was good." But the world he had created did not survive the news of his truancy: his father summoned him to Newburyport for steadying discipline.

The discipline was not uncommon; all of it proved salutary, part of it became sport. It began at five in the morning at the town pump where the boy drank cold water. Then followed a quarter-mile run, a brisk walk, and a swim in the sea. The program of physical culture—calisthenics, running, throwing, swimming, and diving—was complemented by proper diet and plentiful sleep. (The Sullivan boys later enjoyed similar ordeals as members of an athletic club on the Calumet River. But more significant, perhaps, is Sullivan's comment that from the experience of seeing his father swimming naked, he had "a vision of . . . naked mighty men, with power to do splendid things with their bodies.") And when the father became aware of the emotional-mystical tendencies of his son, a less strenuous discipline was added—that of visiting the shipyard and learning how men in the real world work together for great practical ends.

The mystical child had long dreamed of power and worshipped mighty men, but he was suddenly shocked by the presentiment that power, heretofore good, might be evil. This presentiment came during a family picnic in an idyllic spot on the Merrimack River. The boy had wandered alone downstream, dreaming of his little world at South Reading—his meadow, his slender elm and great ash—and lost in the thought that he was now in a larger world "too great for his little size, too bewildering for his untutored mind." Absorbed, he had ascended a hill and entered a dark wood. "Meanwhile something large, something dark was approaching unperceived; something ominous, something sinister that silently aroused him to a sense of its presence. . . . What was it? He could not quite see; he could not make out; except that it was huge, long and dark. . . . The dark thing came ever nearer, nearer in the stillness, became broader, looming, and then it changed itself into full view— an enormous terrifying mass that overhung the broad river from bank to bank." The Amesbury chain mail suspension bridge, with its massive stone towers, its chains and aerial span, evoked images of monsters, giants, and the evils of the fairy world. The boy was seized by dread, from which the father, with his patient and simple explanations, finally released him. Fear was replaced by awe and love: the bridge was transformed into a glorious image of man's beneficent power. But an awareness of the sinister possibilities of technology remained. Natural objects and phenomena had never so impressed him. Perhaps in this recollection Sullivan was imaginatively right in associating nature with the intimate world of the child and technology with a larger, more incomprehensible, intrusive world—that, after all, was a possible account of the nineteenth century. And here, in tree and bridge, were the symbols of the two worlds of romantic nature and mechanical science that he was to try to reconcile. The "aggressive" scientific solutions of engineers that he later admired in the Eads and Dixville bridges had to serve the larger vision of the imaginative artist: technology might become sinister if not guided by the heart.

Sullivan's boyhood (separated from childhood by his eighth birthday) was spent in the city, with summer interludes at the farm. In 1863-64, he spent a bleak winter in Halifax, where his father had opened a dancing school; in the spring of 1864, he returned to the farm; and in the fall he resumed his education at the Brimmer School in Boston. The effect of this change, he says, was disastrous: "As one might move a flourishing plant from the open to a dark cellar, and imprison it there. . . . He mildewed; and the leaves and buds of ambition fell from him." School, with its "sanctioned repressions and routines," was still a prison. The teacher for whom he yearned, one who might liberate him from aimlessness, never came. Dime novels and romances of outdoor adventure fed his fancy. As he explored his new environment, he sensed in it a new power, and between this power and the power he had seen in the movement of the seasons he felt "a great mysterious contrast"—one which defines his later movements between Chicago and the cottage at Ocean Springs, the structure of *Kindergarten Chats,* and the psychological content he gave to "feudal" and "democratic." "In the open all was free, expansive, and luminous," he explains. "In the city all was contraction, density, limitation, and a cruel concentration."

A favorable result of his city excursions was a growing interest in architecture. By the time he was twelve, buildings had acquired personalities, and one in particular—the Masonic Temple at Tremont and Boylston Streets—enamored him and became a city surrogate for the elm. The architect who made buildings "out of his head" (Sullivan uses Ruskin's words to reverse Ruskin's view of originality) now became the quintessential man of power, and with characteristic determination the boy announced that he wished to be one. His father agreed and promised help. Thus when the family made its last move, to

Chicago in 1868, the boy was left behind with his grandparents.[8] He was to complete his education and make a career.

With this in mind, but perhaps as much because he was now free, at the farm again, and pleased with the new Rice Grammar School building, he worked with unusual intensity. He became aware of books as "tools of the mind." In grammar, he passed over the threshold between rote and understanding, and realized the plastic, fluent, living power of language. He also found that he could write well of his own experiences. But the curriculum was seldom "romantic" or relevant: "The history book did not interest him greatly because the people described did not seem human like the people he knew, and the story was mostly about wars." The accent and the complaint were those of Huck Finn, just as the heroism of the boy's daily journey from the farm to the city was an accepted thing "in the days long since gone by." He survived both, and in June 1870 was graduated with honors.

Boyhood passed into adolescence during the summer of 1870. The passage was depicted by a journey to the West, by the expansive geography of an opening world, and by a love affair. Grandfather List wanted to visit his daughter Jennie who lived in Lyon Falls, New York, and Louis was permitted to accompany him. It was the boy's first trip, artfully used by the narrator as an apologue of sudden growth, but also to represent his life-long habit of studying out the land. In the Berkshires, he first experienced mountains—and sublimity. For him the train surmounting the hills enacted a drama of power in which technology (still a giant) was beneficent: "man, in his power . . . had entered the regioned sanctity of these towering hills and like a giant . . . had held them in the hollow of his hand. He had made a path, laid the rails, builded the engines that others might pass." The Hudson River at Albany did not impress him, and the bridge that crossed it he felt was servile and mean. "Why," the narrator asks in the guise of the boy, "could not a bridge perform its task with pride?" And the answer was that of the narrator who had once asked a similar question about sky-scrapers: "He keenly felt that man's amazing power to do, should, in all decency and all reason, be coupled with Romance in the deed . . . this venomous bridge was a . . . denial of all that was best in mankind." The Mohawk Valley stilled this perturbation. The world suddenly opened in an expanse of low hills, and to the boy the works of man seemed small before this revelation of the power of earth. After a night in Utica, whose "settled complacence" differed in kind and quality from that of New England, they went on to Lyon Falls, a dismal village "in true American style, in the prevailing genius of ugliness. . . ."

On the trip Grandfather List told the boy of the developing character traits he had watched from infancy and warned him of the dangers of adolescence. He did not have in mind Minnie Whittlesey, but rather the boy's idea of power which he felt might, in that period of change, be fixed for destruction as well as good. In an age of gentility, Minnie, a young lady of eighteen, was not to be feared. And if love is a power, its sublimation here, in what is one of Sullivan's profoundest memories, should show how equally destructive forces might be suppressed or trans-formed. Minnie dominated her cavalier; she read him Tennyson and Byron; she expressed herself freely in the wonderfully un-guarded intimacy of youth; and she conquered by love. But the relationship was hardly erotic: Minnie played Mary Jane to his Huck Finn. The narrator says that she was "the only truly hu-man he had ever known"; "she had come . . . out of the in-visible . . . to be his faerie queen." And when he adds that "now it seems as though a half a century had stood still," one wonders at both the depth of his romantic sentiment and the evidence of its fixation.

Of course he was not quite fourteen. He was as ready to un-dergo the manly wilderness experience of Brown's Tract as he was to play games of chivalry. He had been partly prepared for the primeval forest by his reading in Mayne Reid and Fenimore

Cooper, and he welcomed the invitation of two farm boys to go along with them. The ten-day trip was arduous and memorable; Sullivan describes it briefly but with an immediacy that reminds one of Thoreau's *The Maine Woods*. It meant much to him: it was obviously formative, a necessary part of the education of an *American* architect. He drew on it again in the seventeenth chapter of *Kindergarten Chats*. It was the climax of a summer which in turn had climaxed all his previous experiences out-of-doors. Such experiences, he maintained, "provided deep and sound foundation for the masterful free spirit, striding in power, in the open. . . ."

The boy became aware of this power within himself when, in the fall of 1870, he at last encountered a teacher who showed him that true freedom lay in the discipline of power. Henri List's concern for the boy he had let alone "for fear of meddling with nature's work" was not groundless but needless. Moses Woolson, a master at the Boston English High School, harnessed Louis' powers.

Woolson, who enters history only in the *Autobiography,* was Sullivan's first true teacher—and the greatest. Teaching was for him a sacred calling, and to its responsibilities he held accountable both himself and his pupils. He taught them a discipline of silence, strict attention, alertness, listening (the whole man engaged in hearing), observation, reflection, and discrimination —in Sullivan's words, *"Self Discipline of self power."* He opened many subjects to them: the symbolism of algebra and the exactitude of geometry;[9] the mysteries of mineralogy and botany—the relationship of function and structure; the imaginative reaches of English literature. He explained the idea of culture—the expression of the genius or inmost self of a people —and recommended Taine's *English Literature.* He introduced his pupils to Asa Gray's *School and Field Book of Botany* (Sullivan's constant guide) and to Gray himself. Much that Sullivan attributes to Woolson, especially the psychology of his discipline, was possibly the result of Sullivan's own ripened psychology (see "Natural Thinking"). But the impact of this pugnaciously devoted man was tremendous. Sullivan modelled himself after him, especially in *Kindergarten Chats* where he dramatized the relationship of student and teacher. For Woolson "stood forth not alone a man but a TEACHER of the young." [10]

The year with Woolson was the most crucial in Sullivan's development. At twelve he had been "scatter-brained"—"rich in impulse but devoid of order, of form, of intention." Now, at fourteen, the best in him, his powers of thought, feeling, and action, had been nurtured and concentrated. He had been formed, and he was prepared to go on successfully, even though the way of his further education was devious.

The year had not been entirely fortunate. Grandmother List died in April 1871. The farm was sold, and Henri List went to Philadelphia to live with his son. The boy remained behind with the John Tompsons, who owned the neighboring farm. George Tompson, his boyhood friend, was now studying engineering at the Massachusetts Institute of Technology; he encouraged Sullivan, whose second year at the English High School was marred by the "virtuous routine" of a conventional schoolmaster, to enter "Tech" immediately. Sullivan passed the entrance examinations, and in the fall of 1872 his formal professional training, which was to be equally brief, began.

One result of living with the Tompsons was that Sullivan's architectural education was complemented by an education in music. John Tompson, who also taught the boy something of good living, introduced him to oratorios. Sullivan responded ecstatically, for here was further evidence of man's power: the composer brought forth music "from nothingness." (Sullivan shared with Whitman the rapture of listening to the human voice. Music and architecture joined in his ornament, and it is fitting that in the Auditorium Building architecture made a home for music.) But John Tompson dispelled "the music-world

of enchantment wherein simple faith had been the true substance and value . . . by substituting . . . a world of fact and
technique." In the narrative of education he represents intellect without the vitalizing power of imagination; he famil-
iarized Sullivan with "the cultural world . . . of intellectual
dissection," with theory, words, the "tyranny of rules." A
similar education—or miseducation—was going on at "Tech."

The school of architecture at "Tech" was new, having been
opened in 1865, but the teaching was old and imported. Its professor, William R. Ware of Ware & Van Brunt, the architects of
Memorial Hall in Cambridge, had studied with Richard Hunt,
the first American to be trained at the École des Beaux Arts.
Ware's assistant, who did most of the actual teaching, was a
recent École graduate, a student of Emil Vaudremer. They
taught the five orders of architecture and the historical styles,
a "misch-masch of architectural theology," according to Sullivan. Sullivan's actual revulsion at this "cemetery of orders and
of styles" is corroborated by his lecture notes, which begin carefully but end abruptly after twenty-two pages—perhaps about
the time he began to turn his attention to the tower of the New
Brattle Street Church by Richardson. The fault he found with
this training is suggested in his characterization of Ware as "not
imaginative enough to be ardent." For Ware, in spite of the
fact that he later helped Sullivan secure his largest commission,
represented not only the traditional architectural teaching but
the Brahmin notion of culture against which Sullivan's life was
a vociferous rebellion.

Sullivan finished the academic year and then turned to Philadelphia. He found employment as a draftsman with the firm of
Furness & Hewitt, whose work attracted him. George Hewitt, a
genteel Anglophile who did "Victorian Gothic in its pantalettes,"
was not responsible for the bold and fresh buildings of the firm.
They were the work of Frank Furness, the son of the Reverend
William Henry Furness, Emerson's life-long friend. Furness was

an original; contemptuous of schools, adapting many styles freely, he did indeed make up buildings out of his head. Sullivan, who admired Furness and enjoyed the quiet atmosphere of the office, learned much during this first apprenticeship,[11] but unfortunately the panic of 1873 terminated it. (He did not understand the nature of financial panics then nor twenty years later when another panic brought about the dissolution of his partnership with Adler. He was to learn from Veblen's *The Theory of Business Enterprise* how panics were created. Thus the run on the banks in 1873 that he witnessed from an office window was, in retrospect, appalling. Like most of the crises he records, it originated in the East.) He went West, to his family in Chicago.

In 1873 Chicago was a city of three hundred thousand people, emerging from its own recent catastrophe, the fire of 1871. Sullivan, who later studied its history and surveyed the cityscape and landscape, called it a "garden city." This city—and with it the possibility of a democratic community—had, he believed, "gone forever with the flames." For with the fire he dated the beginning of a new era of commercial empire. Intent on being big, the new city remained raw and crude; architectural firms built hastily and measured their work by the mile; the steeples that had adorned the skyline were eclipsed; and though the prairie and lake remained to challenge civic vision, "the city lay stretched out, unseemly as a Caliban."

This city, and others like it, was the setting of Sullivan's architectural triumphs. Doubling its population every decade, it sprawled at the circumference and piled up at the center— the "Loop"—which became in the next twenty years "the center of architectural development not merely for the United States but for the whole world." [12] Sullivan, at first dismayed by its ugliness, later came to identify his own sense of power with the drama of power and will in which he found himself. He believed that the men rebuilding Chicago had "vision"; he admired a proud people who "undertook to do what they willed and what they dreamed." Long after the city was rebuilt he was to question this vision.

Among the prominent builders of the new city was Major William Le Baron Jenney, Louis' first employer. An engineer during the Civil War, Jenney was to have a significant part in the rise of the Chicago School; but apparently he impressed Sullivan only as a *bon vivant.*[13] In Jenney's office, however, Louis met a teacher whose influence was as opportune and perhaps as great as that of Moses Woolson—John Edelmann, the foreman.

Like Woolson, Edelmann seems to have no history except that which Sullivan records. His name never appears in the proceedings of the local architectural societies, even though for a time he had set up as an architect. Sullivan, who once wrote that "my reputation as an architect will always be inferior to his," [14] perhaps accounts for Edelmann's failure to succeed when he characterizes him as a drifter. Drift he did, from firm to firm, from architecture to farming; but the fact that he also drifted in the realms of thought—and liked to talk and instruct—made him an exciting teacher. He was twenty-four, seven years older than Sullivan, whom he seems to have made his companion and protégé. Sullivan notes that Edelmann talked on greenback currency and the single tax, that he knew philosophy ("the highest transcendentalisms of German metaphysics"), psychology, and social theory. He introduced Louis to Carlyle and Wagner and to the German culture of Chicago. He extended Sullivan's idea of function, first glimpsed in the study of botany, by explaining his own theory of suppressed functions—the psychological and metaphysical origins of the pressures (as Sullivan also called functions) that necessitate forms. Equally important, he brought Louis to the Lotos Club on the Calumet River, where Louis shared Edelmann's boathouse. Sullivan recalls that he was "wild with joy over this new life."

Neither Edelmann nor Sullivan was among the best or the most dedicated of the athletes who composed the Lotos Club, and they often took time for more education. Sullivan does not mention these outdoor discourses in the *Autobiography* or that although he owed his sense of responsibility as a teacher to Woolson, he owed the mode of instruction (employed in *Kindergarten Chats*) to Edelmann. This more vital education was recorded in the notebook Sullivan had kept at "Tech." In it are sketches and studies by both Edelmann and Sullivan, and a list of books—proposed by Edelmann[15]—which provided Sullivan with a general education in poetry, fiction, science and physical hygiene. The books by Spencer, Jevons, and Tyndall mark the beginning of his wide reading in the science of his day.

The nature of the discourses is perhaps best represented by two dialogues—two essays in which Edelmann answers the questions of his "parasitical" pupil. In one, discussing the problem of indigenous art, Edelmann derides patriotic nationalism and turns instead to the fundamental question of the nature of art. Art, he says, is "noble thought nobly expressed . . . the idea, and not mere representation, is what gives permanent value to an art production." (Sullivan later treated fundamental problems similarly, as in the debates on "styles"; and if idea becomes the idea of a personality, Edelmann's definition of art is also his.) The other essay, prompted by the question of decoration, is a learned discussion of unity ("the power of seeing relations" granted only to the "highest minds") and of the relationship between the development of art and religion. All this Sullivan must have had in mind when he spoke of Edelmann's unrivalled psychological discernment, for although Edelmann's pedagogy was as old as that of Socrates, its practice was new in the 1870's.

The education at the Lotos Club enclosed still another, and the briefest. In July 1874, Sullivan embarked for England, his ultimate destination the École des Beaux Arts in Paris. This was his only voyage to Europe, and his comments on it have a characteristic American ambivalence. The English landscape, with its "ripened" quality, with "the softness, the velvet, the down of age and tradition," was a "finished land";[16] it was solid where America was flimsy. London spoke to him differently, of "massive oldness," and the wretches in the Haymarket shocked him quite as much as those of Liverpool had Melville. His final impression seems to have been one of "tightness." But then he found affinities—at least in retrospect—between London and Boston; and Paris, which he took to eagerly, seems to have had an affinity with Chicago. Its people reminded him of "his own people" in the Middle West. Its spirit was youthful rather than old—drawn from the "child-happiness" he witnessed in the Luxembourg Gardens, and which for the philosopher of the child was "the child-key to France." [17]

Sullivan's success in passing the entrance examinations of the École prefigures his later victories at home. No other portion of the *Autobiography* is so heady, none so apparently without reticence. The narrator, of course, relived one of the supreme tests of youth and recaptured it: how an innocent boy in a flannel suit, white cap, and white canvas shoes not only became a proper dandy (with "infant beard"), but how in six weeks' time he overcame his poor preparation in French, history, and mathematics, to emerge victorious from the three weeks' ordeal of testing that followed.

The vainglory is excusable because it is justified; his achievement was tribute to the mental discipline and physical regimen he had learned from Woolson and his father. And perhaps it was an unconscious attempt to surpass Richardson, whose earlier success at the Beaux Arts Mrs. Rennselaer had praised so highly.

This is suggested by the fact that Richardson's education at the Beaux Arts was of longer duration. Sullivan leaves in doubt the length of his stay. It would have been anticlimactic had he admitted, after the breath-taking account of the examinations, that he remained at the Beaux Arts for only one term. And for an architect who had ridiculed academic training, such an admission would have weakened his position—for only those who succeed can criticize with impunity. Instead he fills the chapter with an account of his own self-education.

Something of what he learned at the Beaux Arts can be seen in the drawings he did for a three-month *projet*—the only one he completed in the atelier of Emil Vaudremer.[18] What he learned in the Latin Quarter is adequately conveyed by a letter to his brother ("The can-can . . . in ordinary clothes is simply disgusting. . . .")[19] and discredits Frank Lloyd Wright's repeated assertion that Sullivan acquired bad habits—perhaps even more—in Paris. He learned much from his preparation in mathematics under M. Clopet: to begin a demonstration with a personal assertion (the method of *Kindergarten Chats*), to be fearful of abstractions and the rigidities of logic and yet to delight in mathematical imagination, and—the goal of his own search for an architectural law—to find a law *"so broad as to admit of* NO EXCEPTION!" By this time he seems to have learned to vivify history and to interpret it in his mature fashion, for he not only gave dramatic accounts of Biblical and Renaissance history, but also remarked to his examiner that he had no sympathy with Roman civilization, that he felt "out of touch with a civilization whose glory was based on force." [20] He devoted much of his time to museums and architectural excursions, and he continued his reading, chiefly in the history of art and music. Taine's books proved the most important: *The Philosophy of Art* and the studies of art in Greece, Italy, and the Netherlands in which Taine exemplified his sociological method and reiterated his major idea, that art reflects the life of a people.[21]

Taine also prompted Sullivan's trip to Italy, a trip undertaken presumably in order to test the critic's assertion that the "Last Judgment" in the Sistine Chapel was done on *momentum*.[22] But it was not so much Italy to which Sullivan responded as it was the genius and personality of Michelangelo. In the presence of the work of the "first mighty craftsman" the boy and the narrator merge as nowhere else in the *Autobiography*. Here was "the glorified man" of his childhood dream: the super-man he had later read of in Nietzsche; the yea-sayer of Carlyle; "the free spirit of man striding abroad in the open" of Whitman. Here, he says, he learned conclusively that imagination surpasses reason. Here, for the first time, he speaks explicitly of the *"beneficence of power."* Here all the impressions of his youth in nature merge in a revelation of the nature and vocation of art. And here, after many pages without the refrain, he significantly concludes with *"There was a Child went forth every day."*

Undoubtedly this was the overwhelming experience of his months in Europe. Sullivan wisely uses it to crystallize his mature conception of man, history, and architecture—that architecture is not fixed, but "a continuous outpouring never to end, from the infinite fertility of man's imagination, evoked by his changing needs." And it is with this conception in mind that he explains his misgivings about the Beaux Arts—its "artificiality," its lack of "primal inspiration." In 1904, he wrote Claude Bragdon that, unlike many other American architects, he was favorably educated at the Beaux Arts because he had absorbed its best principles: the theory of plan; an intellectualized or manipulative, yet valuable notion of function and form; the value of logical thought. And he explains briefly what the *Autobiography* explains at length, why the Beaux Arts' education did not corrupt him as it had others: "The school did not give me my start. My real start was made, when, as a very young child living much out of doors, I received impressions from the shifting aspects of nature so deep, so penetrating, that they have persisted to this day. . . . Hence I entered the school with a certain fixed mental attitude . . . and with a certain vague consciousness and will that someday I must inevitably express myself in my own way. French logic doubtless helped to focus this ambition." [23]

In the spring of 1875 Sullivan returned to Chicago and resumed his education at the Lotos Club. Stimulated by the Beaux Arts and by the technical innovations of men like Frederick Baumann,[24] who had recently solved the problem of the spongy local soil by using isolated pier foundations, he turned to engineering and science. He studied Trautwine's *Engineer's Pocket Book* and eagerly followed in the *Railway Gazette* the weekly progress of the Eads and Dixville bridges. He recognized the honest functionalism of these strictly scientific structures and appreciated them as examples of beneficent power. ("The idea of spanning a void appealed to him as masterful in thought and deed"—the engineer was almost as god-like as Michelangelo.) And he went on to master the scientific method because he now saw in it a needed "power of solution." At the same time he widened his scientific horizons by reading Darwin and other evolutionists. Finally, in John W. Draper's popular *The Intellectual Development of Europe,* with its contrasts between ages of faith and ages of reason, he found the fundamental polarity of his own historical thought—that of constraining feudalism and liberating democracy; and he found science (for Draper himself was a scientist, albeit a typical Victorian one who desired faith) placed in the vanguard of freedom.

Meanwhile he was making his architectural career as a draftsman and decorator. In the winter of 1875-76, Edelmann, who had gone into partnership with Joseph Johnston, employed Sullivan to design the frescoes for the Sinai Synagogue at Indiana Avenue and Twenty-First Street; and in the spring of 1876, Edelmann set him to work on the more controversial frescoes of the Moody Tabernacle. The first commission probably brought Sullivan to the attention of Dankmar Adler, for Adler is said to have designed the Synagogue. The second commission, much discussed by a wary congregation and commented on in the newspaper, brought the nineteen-year-old artist wider notice.[25]

The firm of Johnston & Edelmann, however, did not survive these depression years. In 1877, Edelmann went to Iowa to farm. Sullivan turned to other jobs, and by judicious moves made his way upward. Still it was Edelmann's interest that finally brought him to Adler's attention, for Edelmann introduced Sullivan to Adler in 1878 (1879?) when he returned to work in the offices of Burling & Adler. When Adler established his own firm in 1879, Edelmann again forwarded his protégé. Adler, twelve years older than Louis, was well-established, with a clientele of solid Jewish and German merchants. He had had engineering experience during the Civil War, and was respected in the profession for his engineering skill and leadership. He needed a designer. In 1879, he engaged Sullivan, who proved his abilities in the design of the Central Music Hall, the Borden residence, and the Borden Block. The kindly, patriarchal Adler, to whom Sullivan owed much and whom he repays in affectionate tribute in the *Autobiography,* soon suggested partnership.

The partnership, entered into in 1881, climaxes the *Autobiography.* Now "a full-fledged architect before the world," Sullivan felt that at last he could begin to embody his "sane philosophy of . . . living architecture. . . ." This philosophy was founded on a law that he had rediscovered for himself in the study of nature—that *form follows function.* But it was his genius to realize that this law of vital expression had an even wider application. In the years that followed, during which he unfolded the idea, he not only used it as a tool of social and historical analysis, he extended and deepened it, making of it a philosophy of "Man and his powers" and a gospel of democracy.

2: THE MUSES OF EUROPE

To discuss architecture and ignore life is frivolous.
Louis Sullivan (1905)

In 1837, during a period of fervid nationalism, Ralph Waldo Emerson delivered an address on "The American Scholar" before the Phi Beta Kappa society at Cambridge. Having already offered in *Nature* (1836) a philosophy of nature and man with which to liberate American culture and to further the originality of the American artist, he now proclaimed: "Mr. President and Gentlemen, this confidence in the unsearched might of man belongs, by all motives, by all prophecy, by all preparation, to the American Scholar. We have listened too long to the courtly muses of Europe. The spirit of the American freeman is already suspected to be timid, imitative, tame. Public and private avarice make the air we breathe thick and fat. The scholar is decent, indolent, complaisant." [1]

In 1843, in "American Architecture," Horatio Greenough wrote: "We have heard the learned in matters relating to art express the opinion that these United States are destined to form a new style of architecture. Remembering that a vast population, rich in material and guided by the experience, the precepts, and the models of the Old World, was about to erect durable structures for every function of civilized life, we also cherished the hope that such a combination would speedily be formed." But, he added, "We forgot that, though the country was young, yet the people were old. . . . We forgot that the Republic had leaped fullgrown . . . from the brain of her parent. . . . We forgot that reason had been the dry nurse of the great offspring. . . ." He noted that "in our eagerness to appropriate, we have neglected to adapt, to distinguish—nay, to understand" that though America had "called from the vasty deep of the past the spirits of the Greek, the Roman, and the Gothic styles . . . they would not come when she did call to them!" And he advised: "Let us encourage experiment at the risk of license. . . . Let us consult nature, and in the assurance that she will disclose a mine richer than was ever dreamed of by the Greeks, in art as well as in philosophy." [2]

In 1870, the Reverend William Henry Furness delivered the final address at the fourth annual convention of the American Institute of Architects. He spoke of the "blood-relationship of Architecture to Nature," and cited for support the fourth stanza of Emerson's "The Problem," with its suggestive lines:

> For out of Thought's interior sphere
> These wonders rose to upper air . . .

Perhaps with his son's work in mind, he said that "it is an adventurous thing in this land to set before us anything of which we cannot at once tell what to think"; and in a kind of muted Emersonianism he reminded the architects that inspiration was still available and that "the weary age of imitation will come to an end. . . ." His concluding remarks were directly to the point: "We are building now of Iron, and we require new styles of building fitted to this material, so that Iron shall have its honest credit and publish its massive strength. . . . Shall this homely, stolid substance have its rights . . . will it not demand—will it not create, new orders of architecture?" [3]

In 1886, at the third annual convention of the Western Association of Architects, Dankmar Adler delivered the presidential address. "How great is the privilege granted us," he said, "in being part, not of a Renaissance, but of a naissance in architecture. For there is surely being born into our world a new style, the style of America, the style of the civilization of the nineteenth century, developed by its wants, its conditions and limitations, and nurtured by the best there is in the lives of you whom I see before me. . . ." The development of this architecture he compared favorably to the rise of an American literature in the age of Emerson—an age now passing away but whose inspiration, in an era of even greater challenge, the infant architecture inherited: "Great and glorious as was the rise of American literature, the development of American architecture is still more wonderful."

John Wellborn Root, Adler's confrere, addressed a dinner meeting of the same convention. "We, living in the full light of the nineteenth century, freed from the thralldom of even our less fortunate brothers across the sea, we men of the Western Association of Architects can do what we please. . . . This is the age, and this the country of the great architectural go-as-you-please. I know of but one grave difficulty which besets us. This is the answering of the question, so constantly asked, 'What is the style of that house?' " Root named the possible styles of the past twenty years: the "Victorian Cathartic . . . in full flower in the London law courts"; the "Tubercular Style," better known as Queen Anne; the "Cataleptic . . . supposed to have originated in New England, in the last century"; the "Dropsical," a very popular current style often called Romanesque. He asked the architects to act to remedy the diseases of style.

At the same convention, Sullivan read an "Essay on Inspiration." [4]

The rise of the Chicago School was proclaimed by new means and methods of construction, such as the isolated pier and the floating foundation, the steel-frame and the "Chicago window"—by what came to be called "Chicago construction." For the emergence of new means and methods are, according to Giedion, the "constituent facts" that indicate a new architectural tradition. Ideas, however, are equally constituent. New means and methods may be adopted with limited awareness; every building employing them is not necessarily architecture. Without ideas, without broader intellectual traditions than those of architecture, new forms for functions and feelings do not emerge. Only vital intelligence creates new forms. Such intelligence is the mark of genius and a fruit of tradition.

Of course the Chicago School arose in response to immediate conditions and needs. Adler, for example, acknowledged this when he spoke of "the era of material prosperity which followed the rapid development of our railroad, our telegraph and industrial systems since the close of the war of rebellion." [5] Chicago became a center of trade and transportation; the office building, the hotel, the department store, the warehouse were visible results.

The conditions that stimulated new building also stimulated new ideas; there were other Chicago Schools besides that of architecture: the new sociology, the new education, the new psychology. These contempory trends many architects overlooked. But even the most insular architect could not escape the intellectual ferment at work within his own discipline. The professional journals carried news of ideas and the professional societies discussed them. They did so eagerly and earnestly out of a need for education, and building and discussion went hand-in-hand, furthered by daily intimacy.

The Chicago School did not become aware of itself as a school until 1883, when *The Inland Architect and Builder* was established under the leadership of R. C. McLean. McLean edited a magnificently illustrated monthly journal with which the most able and articulate Chicago architects were closely associated— Root and Sullivan were special contributors for many years. And although there had been a Chicago chapter of the American Institute of Architects as early as 1869, McLean urged and promoted the formation of the Western Association of Architects in 1884. *The Inland Architect* became the official organ of the new association, and rightly: both were concerned with architecture "in the West."

Chicago builders had not always distinguished between building and architecture, nor had they felt the need for an independent architectural society. That they did after the Civil War was due to the renewed cultural consciousness and aspiration of their increasingly productive region. Before the Civil War, the single expression of the desire for cultural parity with the East had been the demand for a "Western" literature. In opposing American reliance on English literature, Eastern literary patriots had looked to the West for a native art. The West, however, had not been ready to fulfill these expectations. Nevertheless, the Western agrarian democratic sentiment and cultural irreverence toward the East remained—intensified, after the Civil War, by the economic and cultural exploitation of the East.

The arguments for this Western culture were not new. They had been fashioned by literary nationalists a half-century earlier —that is why "Western" and "American" became synonymous. Emerson and Whitman had emboldened the American to cast off servility to Europe; populists in art now urged a similar liberation from the genteel, Europeanized East. Hamlin Garland, for example, reintroduced Emerson's and Whitman's cultural program in his iconoclastic *Crumbling Idols,* a manifesto published just after the World's Fair of 1893. Its rebelliousness was the characteristic expression of a generation at war with tradition. "Rise, O young man and woman of America!" he exhorts. "Stand erect! . . . Turn your back on the past . . . in justice to the future. Cease trying to be correct, and become creative. This is our day. The past is not vital. . . . Libraries do not create great poets and artists. . . ." Turn instead, he advises, to nature; accept the realities of your region, even the ugly and common; create in the "image of life." Here, however, the architectural movement anticipated the literary one: a decade earlier Chicago architects had proclaimed similar things.[6]

The earlier and later proponents of American culture were linked by a more important bond than the repudiation of tradition—the appeal to an organic art. Most of the architects of the Western Association were workaday men who adhered to styles because of taste. They agreed with William Mundie who respected the past and was sick of "the hackneyed subject of an American style. . . ."[7] When they yielded it was only to the extent of accepting the Richardsonian Romanesque as the most worthy style for American building. Like many of the literary nationalists of Emerson's day who sought originality by accommodating American themes to borrowed forms, they were willing to discover among the styles one readily adapted to American needs. Nevertheless, the major spokesmen of the Western Association championed organic principles. The development of an organic tradition in American architecture was primarily their work (they did not know the writings of Horatio Greenough). Many of the ideas that underlay the formula, "form follows function"—ideas usually attributed to Sullivan and which he arrogated to himself—were the common property of the Chicago School.

All were aware of the necessity of building in response to living, contemporaneous needs. Allen B. Pond, for example, wrote that "the requirements of American life demand of the architect buildings that shall answer new purposes and meet unwonted uses under conditions never before presented to the craft." Root translated Gottfried Semper who had prophesied that a "real national art" will spring up first in America: "Style is the conformity of an art object with the circumstances of its origin and the conditions and circumstances of its development." And speaking for himself he said: "Our architecture if it is good will fit us—every part of us. . . ." W. W. Clay believed that the structural elements of a building should be honestly revealed; and Root claimed that in a building "the force with which . . . function is expressed measures its value as a work of art." Truth of this kind, he realized, was the one quality the age demanded of art. The organic principles valued in an age of science were use, fitness, truth.

The honest use of structure was not limited simply to utilitarian ends. The Chicago School acknowledged a natural law of fitness: the outward must express and serve inner needs. Pond spoke of "integral verities" and explained that "Spencer, the realist, and Emerson, the idealist, each affirm that the nature of the inner man determines the outer . . . that the spirit molds the body." Buildings had souls—"The plan, the purpose, the inner soul of the building, determine the exterior, its forms and features. . . ." And buildings, to be living things, demanded a unity like that of natural forms, a unity that was expressed in the part and in the whole because it grew out of singleness of purpose and fidelity to function. This unity, maintained Frederick Baumann, the German intellectual of the Chicago School, respected even the ideal—artistic expression. He cited Wilhelm Lübke's *History of Architecture* to support his belief that ornament was not subordinate to but integral with structure: "This genius enrobes his creation . . . [so] as to enable him to disclose before the eyes of all, the ground plan and construction in language of form such as is beautiful and clear to general understanding; and by means of proper membering, to pose the building object in the light of a live organism which establishes even its ornamentation as though sprung from the power of a natural law."

Such organic considerations replaced the question of styles with the more generic question of style, and style, in turn, gave way to the individual solution of new problems. As Root said of style: "It is inherent—a thing of the head and heart, not of the epidermis . . . the life and existence of the work." The question of an American style was now deferred in the hope that such a style might eventually emerge from the converging solutions of a generation of architects whose common bond was a broad sympathy with the spirit of the time. Based on what Sullivan, in his first address, called a "more rational and organic mode of expression," these solutions were to distinguish the architects of the Chicago School from the more literary and eclectic architects of the East.[8]

To demand that architects build organically is one thing; to teach them how is another. Sullivan did both, but teaching was eminently his vocation. Like Emerson, he reminded a generation of the fundamental sources of originality in man and nature. He spoke directly to the problem of inspiration; he wished to quicken those men whom Emerson had called "the dead alive." Like Whitman, he felt that one must accept the open possibilities of democracy and nourish one's art in the warm flow of human life. He spoke for the heart, and urged his associates to acquire a democratic sentiment, an all-absorbing sympathy for the people to whom they were responsible.

In proposing an organic art he wanted something more than a native art characterized by a national style. He wanted a new way of thinking, feeling, and expressing—that is, a *man* constituted for democracy, truly worthy of his place and moment. And when he opposed "styles" something more than patriotism was at stake. Styles represented the "past," "dead" forms, and "repressive" authority. To oppose them was to demand genuine freedom to live and to be.

He did not promulgate a rule. "Form follows function" is not a rule, but the brief statement of a complex vision. "With me, architecture is not an art," he told Bragdon, "but a religion, and that religion but a part of democracy." His concern was never simply with architecture but with democratic architecture. This made him the poet-seer of the Chicago School and an exponent—along with Dewey, Veblen, Jane Addams, H. D. Lloyd, and Debs—of the vigorous humanism of his generation.[9] And this was why he felt that the "failure" of architecture in the World's Fair of 1893 was also a "betrayal"—a betrayal of democracy.

Almost from the very beginning of his career, Sullivan prescribed a far-reaching program for a national style. When he delivered the essay "Characteristics and Tendencies of American Architecture" before his colleagues in the Western Association in 1885, he was only twenty-nine and not yet well known. He had not yet employed the steel-frame as Jenney had boldly done in the Home Insurance Company Building in 1884. And what he had designed, although fulfilling the need for daylight, was not determinate—was marred, in fact, by his experiments in ornament. Nevertheless he spoke out clearly and authoritatively, and much in the way Melville had used his essay on Hawthorne, used the occasion to declare himself. For his philosophy had already germinated. He was sure of his powers and acutely aware of how they must be disciplined. Veiling references to himself, he spoke of the individual who "from day to day [seeks] expedients by means of which to shape his immediate surroundings into a realization of his desires"; he suggested that the forces impelling the individual might produce significant results; and though the results might not be typical, he claimed that they would still be characteristic. In this way he made himself a "stock-personality" (Whitman's representative man, or what he himself called a "true, normal type") and his discipline policy.

Such tactics were not simply the result of arrogance but rather of Sullivan's consciousness of the problems that underlay the issue of national style. He knew that a distinctly American architecture could not be achieved by grafting or transplanting the architecture of the Old World. He advocated instead a gradual growth on native ground, acknowledging the difficulties of that slow "assimilation of nutriment." Knowing, too, that it would involve a "struggle against obstacles," he looked hopefully to two favoring conditions: he believed, as the transcendentalists had, in the energy of an "unexhausted soil" (a mystique of the soil is a constant element of his thought);[10] and he believed that a new generation would claim its American birthright, the "freedom to receive and assimilate impressions. . . ." From the union of free men and fresh soil, he expected "emotions of rare quality"—results that he felt were the very foundations of art. Thus he discarded the dream of a "Minerva-like" architecture and looked instead for "early signs of a spontaneous architectural feeling arising in sympathy with the emotions latent or conspicuous in our people."

That such generative emotion find expression in architecture was Sullivan's constant plea. He believed that the lack of such emotion was the signal deficiency of most architects. But as he noted here, it was not his deficiency. For one might discover this emotion in an "element of warmth tinging scholastic formalism," and one would certainly meet it in "the efforts of those upon whose imagination the chromatic eloquence of words and of music have taken strong hold," and especially in the creation "of the gifted ones whose souls are finely attuned to the touching beauty of nature and of humanity." The language here, with its suggestion of romantic sensibility—a sensibility fully expressed in the concluding paragraphs of the address—poses Sullivan's problem. He needed most to clearly distinguish between sentimental and vital emotion,[11] and to master the vital by uniting it with logical thought.

He found ample evidence of emotion in our literature, but it was "exquisite . . . not virile." In spite of his own inclination toward romantic sentiment ("Under the influence of its warmth of feeling," Sullivan-the-ornamentalist said, "hard lines flow into graceful curves, angularities disappear in a mystical blending of surfaces.")—indeed because of this inclination, he firmly rejected the genteel. The art of the day seemed to him, as it seemed to Whitman, to be too self-conscious of finish and "minute detail" (see his own buildings), but, above all, to have accepted "a tacit fiction as to the passions." It expressed only "the well-behaved and docile emotions," and was "too much a matter of heart and fingers, and too little an offspring of brain and soul." In the then current language of literary discussion, he wanted strength rather than refinement.

His complaint was also that expressed by Emerson fifty years earlier, that American arts were feminine and characterless, enfeebled for want of the "masculine or creative" because they imitated those of Europe and had not been "called out by the necessity of the people." [12] Sullivan recognized that the masculine emotion he desired, an emotion infusing "glowing vitality into root and stem" and expressing itself in "exuberant foliation," was thwarted by imitation: "we have all been educated to a dependence upon our artistic inheritance." He was convinced that the germ of greatness was within the people. He believed that "our art is for the day" and must answer to popular feeling. And he knew that the struggle was within his own profession, for where such convictions were absent there would be no creating power, and where there was no creating power there would be no "plastic alphabet by means of which to identify our beliefs." He said that as a professional class "architects . . . have held it more expedient to maintain the traditions of their culture than to promulgate vitalizing thought." Had he asked what might be done, his answer would have been Emerson's: "One: redeem them from imitation . . . Two: preach the nature of things."

This is what he tried to do by calling attention to power. In the world of business, he remarked, power did not sit at the feet of Omphale. The businessman heeded the day, and if he used power crudely and harshly, he also used it with the kind of creative logic Sullivan admired. The businessman, he explained, had "the ability to develop elementary ideas organically . . . into subtle, manifold and consistent ramifications. . . ." This power of thought was the "brain" he had mentioned earlier; those emotions vitally generated by the needs of the day were the "soul." Together they would harness crude power. "Subtilized, flushed with emotion and guided by clear insight," power, he affirmed, "is a worker of miracles." [13]

The ability to develop ideas organically was the power he himself needed. The miracle he had prophesied, however, was Richardson's Marshall Field Wholesale Store. Begun early in 1886, this building was the best example of what Sullivan desired. And when, in the ensuing years, its lesson was forgotten, Sullivan repeated it by praising this building as he never praised another. "Here," he told the student in *Kindergarten Chats*, "here is a *man* for you to look at . . . an entire male. . . . Buildings such as this, and there are not many of them, stand as landmarks. . . . Four-square and brown, it stands, in physical fact, a monument to trade, to the organized commercial spirit, to the power and progress of the age, to the strength and resource of individuality and force of character; spiritually, it stands as the index of a mind, large enough, courageous enough to cope with these things, master them, absorb them and give them forth again, impressed with the stamp of large and forceful personality; artistically, it stands as the creation of one who knows well how to choose his words. . . . Therefore have I called it, in a world of barren pettiness, a male; for it sings the song of procreant power, as the others have squealed of miscegenation." [14]

When Sullivan addressed the Western Association again in the following year, he spoke about the nature of things and the elemental sources of his own inspiration. Hoping to redeem his colleagues from imitation, he boldly delivered a long prose-rhapsody, "Essay on Inspiration." This disarmingly sincere and inspired essay was the only address Sullivan recalls in the *Autobiography*, and there, probably thinking of what he had written to Whitman, he said that the convention furnished the "pretext and occasion" for saying something about his deepest thoughts. He remembered that "the effusion did not take" but that years later R. C. McLean had said that it was "his architectural thesis." His pleasure in these recollections was evident; he explained the essay in light of the mature philosophy of the *Autobiography* and reprinted portions of it. And having never received the "surgery" he had asked of Whitman, he supplied it himself: "the work [is] a bit sophomoric, and over-exalted, but the thought is sound." [15]

The thought was not entirely Whitman's, for though Sullivan unknowingly drew from the same transcendental springs, the inspiration was his own. He, too, had enjoyed an original relation to the universe. If the poetry with which he expressed his ecstasy was lamentably sentimental, the emotion that prompted it was nevertheless genuine and overwhelming. He had discovered, he had felt—for one must feel in order to be transformed—the forms-and-functions of life, the rhythms of flowing nature. Later, in *Kindergarten Chats,* where he brilliantly explained his metaphysics, he said: "That which exists in spirit ever seeks and finds its physical counterpart in form, its visible image"; the universe is one "wherein all is function, all is form. . . ." But this principle, this fundamental rhythm of life in nature and man, he admitted, was cause for despair as well as for joy. For it expressed itself in both "the very wedding-march and ceremonial that quickens into song the unison of form and function" and "the dirge of their farewell. . . ." Life *was* growth and decay, organization and dissolution; and a "thought in decadence" was inevitably a "form in decadence," a "living thought, a living form." Stated in terms of light and shadow, his personal problem, accordingly, was, like Thoreau's in *The Service*, not to become an "opaque and moribund . . . man who gives forth . . . a shadow in his daily walk." Wishing to give forth only light, but recognizing the dark seasons of decay, he, too, sought within this very rhythm the warrant of renewal. "I'll make a song of spring," he told the student of the *Chats*, "that shall dispel . . . gloomy wintry skies . . . and make awake to sweet rejuvenance the lark, the soaring singing lark that doth abide within the hearts—of all the young!"

"Inspiration" was that song. In it he first expressed his awareness of the rhythm that was the basis—and the most profound meaning—of his art in building, ornament, and writing. It is the vital structure of his best books; it is the tension of rigid and flowing line in his ornament, and the tension, too, of ornament and structure in his buildings. In fact, even the primary elements of architecture were its symbolic expression. The pier, he explained in *Kindergarten Chats*, balances within itself "the two great forces, the simplest, elemental rhythms of Nature, to wit, the rhythm of growth, of aspiration, of that which would rise into the air: which impulse we shall call the Rhythm of Life: and the counter-rhythm of decadence, of destruction, of that which would crush to the earth, of that which makes for a return to the elements of earth, the Rhythm of Death." The static, timeless character of the pier represents the equilibrium of these forces, but the unstable lintel, raised up by man, represents birth—new life, the emergence of art and value, the power of man. Static forms thus become fluid, responsive to human need. And finally, in the arch, which is the pier-and-lintel in motion, man represents not only his "own ephemeral span" but his acceptance and transcendence of death. For the arch, which is a "crystallization of [the] abyss," is also a triumph over the abyss. It is sublime because it is a form "against Fate."

Sullivan's poem is such an arch. He could sing of life because he accepted death as the condition of life and renewed inspiration. The dialectic of the poem, its movement from spring to fall to questioning of the infinite, enacts his hope, despair, and ultimate serenity. The theme of "Growth: A Spring Song" is the awakening of life, the corresponding awakening of springtime and inspiration in the heart of the poet, and his joy in the present. He sings of an "ever fecund and joyous" nature—like Whitman, his song is of "the procreant urge of the world." [16] "Decadence: Autumn Reverie" is a song of death, of sadness in "reminiscence." Life now returns to the root, and the poet becomes aware of polarities: of growth and decay, light and darkness, harmony and discord, fortune and failure. Night falls, he is disconsolate and enters "the valley of negation"; he confronts his own soul and its shadows and finds blighted lilies, trampled violets, faded illusions, jetsam—all signs of "the slow decay of once fresh spontaneity." Again like Whitman, whose "A Word Out of the Sea" ("Out of the Cradle Endlessly Rocking") and "Elemental Drifts" Sullivan echoed, the poet feels an overwhelming sympathy with death. Yielding to death (and to his unconscious) he discovers, as Whitman had, a new strength; he feels that he will be reborn into "a nobler, greater life. . . ." For he now realizes that life grows out of death, that there is a "delicate chemistry changing poison into vital sap. . . ." Yet his hymn to death, the "Great Denier," is a defiant hymn to negative force, to the "reactionary cause of every change"; death is simply the constant force calling out the "aspiring force" in man. Thus, when the storm comes, he pits his human force against the immensities of fate.

This naturalistic gesture was neither characteristic of Sullivan's response to nature nor a satisfying solution of his metaphysical longings. In the final section of the poem, "The Infinite: A Song of the Depths," he turns to the sea, the image of the infinite and of his own soul, to ponder the meaning of the "unsatisfied song of the Twilight." He wants now to discover the "deep, fluid, comprehending all" beneath life and death—the ultimate serenity. He confesses that he has not understood the promptings of his soul and that he has covered his soul with the "embroidery of long transmitted thought." He seeks an answer from the sea. But when another storm destroys his growing identification with the sea, all he finds afterwards is "jetsam from the wreakage of my hopes." Yet among the debris is "a fragmentary token of serenity divine." The sea, he tells us, has answered his questioning heart, and this revelation, he affirms, is the imperishable seed of mature inspiration. Unlike the inspiration of youth, this seed will grow in all the poet's springtimes and bear witness to his understanding of the depths.

So, too, will the art of the architect. For great and indigenous art, Sullivan concluded, is the fruit of inspiration. When it "tallies" such desires, when it arrests and typifies "in materials the harmoniously interblended rhythms of nature and humanity, sustained by an essence wholly inscrutable, yet manifest as wondrously elusive mobility and abiding serenity," it achieves a mobile equilibrium and reveals "the deepest inspiration and the most exalted reach of art." The poet, he said in the letter to Whitman, resolves "himself into subtle unison with Nature and Humanity" and blends "the soul harmoniously with materials. . . ." He does this by means of his spiritualized senses —by means of an "exquisitely vital sympathy." Failing here, he fails entirely, for even logic, a requisite of art, will then prove sterile. In *Kindergarten Chats*, Sullivan warned the architect that his program, followed without inspiration, would produce a "very prosaic result." "Logic, scholarship, or taste, or all of them combined," he maintained, "cannot make organic architecture." That, too, was the explicit application of his poem. He founded his hopes for an American art on the creative sallies of inspiration. "Spontaneous and vital art," he insisted, "must come fresh from nature, and can only thus come."

This poem was even more clearly a declaration of the discovery of his own vital powers. In it he had plumbed the unconscious, the source of what he later called the subconscious energy of imagination. He spoke in *Kindergarten Chats* of the "moment in our lives when we burst our bonds or fail to burst them." Certainly the conjunction of Whitman and Richardson had produced such a moment. For when Sullivan designed the Auditorium Building during these years, he built a lasting tribute to the men who had liberated him. The tremendous masonry building, strong and clean, rearing its tower proudly, was a monument to Richardson. The murals of the Auditorium theatre, depicting allegorically the themes of his poem, were a memorial to Whitman.[17] In the greatest architect and in the greatest poet of his day, he had found what he had written to Whitman he hoped he would find: "the basis of a virile and indigenous art."

How well Sullivan's associates understood his "effusion" is easily ascertained by subsequent discussions of style and by Sullivan's determination to direct the inquiry to more central problems of creativity. In a discussion of the present tendencies of architectural design in America, Sullivan challenged Root's claims that America must first have a national character before it can have a national style, and that lacking such a national character, it must modify what it already possesses and emulate the spirit of past achievements. "I think we are starting at the wrong end entirely," Sullivan said (speaking extemporaneously). "We are taking the results of what has already passed, examining on the surface, and from that are searching for the source of impulse. I do not believe the origin of style is outside, but within ourselves, and the man who has not the impulse

Photograph by Richard Nickel

The Auditorium Building (1887-89)

Toward a virile and indigenous art

within him will not have the style. But the more he thinks, the more he reflects, observes and assimilates, the more style he will have." This broadside upset the usually genial Root. He replied that he wanted the architect to go after "those original sources from which he took *his* inspiration"; in this way he would produce parallel results. Sullivan responded: ". . . any historic motive . . . now seems rather thin and hollow when used in our designs." [18] That closed the discussion, but not the argument.

In another discussion Sullivan declared that temperament, the product of the organic influences of climate and locality, was "the creator and arbiter of art." Like Taine, whom he was following here, Sullivan in effect was saying: "Let us no longer consider works but artists, that is to say, the way in which artists feel, invent, and produce. . . . In confronting objects the artist must experience *original sensation* . . . born with talent[,] his perceptions . . . are delicate and quick. . . . Through this faculty he penetrates to the very heart of things. . . . This sensation, moreover, so keen and so personal, is not inactive—by a counterstroke the whole nervous and thinking machinery is affected by it. Man involuntarily expresses his emotions . . . you will . . . everywhere find the same inward process . . . we may call it genius or inspiration . . . but if you wish to define it precisely you must always verify therein the vivid spontaneous sensation which groups together the train of accessory ideas, master[s], fashion[s], metamorphose[s] and employ[s] them in order to become manifest." [19]

This was the gist of Sullivan's answer to the question: "What is the just subordination, in architectural design, of details to mass?" The rhythmic nature of climate, he explained, awakens "corresponding sympathies within the heart." [20] Left untrammelled by theory, these sympathies "would spontaneously evolve a coordination of mass and detail, so normal, so indigenous, that it would instinctively be recognized as literally and poetically just." In this process differentiation replaces subordination, for the organic method is one of "expansive and rhythmic growth" in which "a single, germinal impulse or idea . . . permeate[s] the mass and its every detail with the same spirit. . . ." His example was natural growth in trees and leaves— natural, too, as Whitman found animals, because the tree is not "dyspeptic with introspection." He demanded similar spiritual, living results in building, and he insisted that they could only spring from the life of the architect: "On no other basis are results of permanent value to be attained."

When Sullivan recapitulated the discussion, he took his argument directly from Whitman. "I value spiritual results only," he affirmed, "I say spiritual results precede all other results, and indicate them." The problem of style must be treated on "a spiritual or psychic basis"; theory must be put aside; we must begin where Whitman began, with the artist immersed in nature, responsive to the inscrutable pervasive power of life. And, like Whitman, we must remain "unperturbed." We must accept our inspiration, our deepest emotions, but, realizing the inevitable compromise with death, we must also practice "great prudence." The laws of art are within the self; they are the very reflex of the rhythms of nature.

The architects, however, rejected Sullivan's proposals by rejoining either with the cliches of "styles" or the already familiar articles of functionalism. O. J. Pierce, for example, said that "a building with a soul is a work of architecture. . . ." He did not mean by "soul" all that Sullivan did; he simply meant that a building must be unitary and declare its purpose in every part. Insisting on fitness and utility, he separated mass and detail, and maintained that mass was primary. Sullivan himself accepted this as a logical consideration in designing but not as an inspirational one; and though Pierce's distinctions between mass as masculine (strength and power) and detail as feminine (grace, refinement, and beauty) pleased him, he still knew that all that he had meant by differentiation had not been understood.[21]

The process of creation is always difficult to describe. That is why Sullivan finally took the student directly to nature. Meanwhile, hoping for understanding, he talked of "expression," of "the artistic use of the imagination," of "intellectual or objective *vs.* emotional or subjective architecture." In every instance his concern was with the inner sources of expression and with the way in which the soul blends with materials, interfusing objective and subjective, indeed transforming matter into symbols of spirit.

When he next spoke on "Style," his theme was artistic growth as an effort toward such expression. Relinquish mechanical and intellectualistic theories of art, he counseled; free the faculties for normal growth and let them blend with "the more subtle manifestations of emotion." Such growth, he maintained, "evidences at the beginning of its rhythm the objective, and toward maturity, the subjective view." [22] Then consider the soul, "the inscrutable impelling force that determines an organism and its life"; and note its abiding essence or identity. For style (his example was a pine tree) is the "resultant of its identity and its surroundings." Study natural things—"Have you thought much on common and simple things? Has it occurred to you how beautiful and mysterious they really are?" (The questions were Whitman's.) Study their "perfectly spontaneous and unequivocal adjustment of means to end." But realize, finally, that "subtile identity" is the essential condition of style; its "eye" or intuition discerns the truth inherent in all things and its sympathy identifies it with their inner nature, and in this way self— and style—are nurtured. For style, Sullivan always insisted, is the developing seed within the self—the expression of a "consistent and definite expansion of a pronounced individuality. . . ."[23]

Style in this sense requires a discipline more demanding than that of books; it requires self-culture, the nurture of all the faculties and of the sensibility. "Identity" was Whitman's special word, and the discipline of identity that Sullivan elaborated in his next address was Whitman's too. One is identified, becomes the particular individual he is, by his response to things, by the constant intercourse of the "I" (the self) and the "Not-me" (the world). Individuality is therefore natural and inevitable, the child of one's emotional discovery of the world and of what one accepts or rejects. Like every natural process, it is a matter of time, of seed, flower, and fruit—it cannot be hastened or delayed. But the fructifying germ of the emotions can be cultivated; one can willingly touch things with the senses, and with senses quickened by the "heart." Stating his psychology briefly, Sullivan said that "emotion is simply the attention that the heart gives." This he had learned from Whitman; and praising Whitman as good for body and soul, he cited all of "There Was a Child Went Forth." But the discipline of identity had a further moral: responsibility. If the artist is identified by what he receives and assimilates, he is responsible for what he becomes. If his individuality declares itself in expression, it too is judged.[24]

These addresses are a commentary on Sullivan's growth as a man and artist. They were written during his first period of successful building, the period of the Auditorium and the Wainwright Building, and they mark his rise to fame.

Of course there were more wordly signs—election to the Chicago Club, a fashionable home, a fashionable life—for Sullivan eagerly seized the conspicuous rewards of success. In this he was a man of the age. But the cottage he built at Ocean Springs, Mississippi, was for him the sign of something more than affluence. Nothing grieved him more (not even, one feels, the disaster of his marriage) than its dispossession. For it represented nature: it was the "open," his place of inspiration, his garden, a workshop of living forms and ornament.

In *Kindergarten Chats* teacher and pupil survey New York, and here—as Henry James also lamented—"money is God, and God is money. . . ." Chicago, the "city of indifference," is not much better; only its youth, its "I WILL!" holds out hope. Both present the spectacle of "modern American humanity," of "abject spiritual beggary." In spite of their schools, libraries, and art galleries, there is no civilization: there is "CALIBAN!" The indictment is just, but for Sullivan it was an indictment only of the eccentricities of our civilization. He still had faith in the spiritual resources of the country. "Great cities," he believed, "are great battlegrounds . . . whereon strong minds gather together, and clash in the fierce rut of ambition." They breed distraction, noise, turmoil, worry, jostle, wear and tear. But "the vast open country . . . breeds its minds, its hearts, as it brings forth its wheat, its trees, its rains. . . ." The city is "indoors," the country "out-of-doors"; the city is for strife and activity, the country for strength and reanimation. The country, therefore, is the "prime source of power," the city only the place of its dissipation for good or ill. And what he said of city and country also described the activities and needs of his own life. It described the rhythm of creation—influx and efflux, contemplation and action—and the polarity of experience which great men and civilizations harmonize.

This profound awareness of the region as the "source of the power of the great cities" and of the need to be in touch with "the simple, the natural, the human" might have made Sullivan a city planner had he lived today. But city planning in his day was usually of the kind exemplified in the projects of Daniel Burnham. It complemented the Renaissance classic architecture of the World's Fair; and though the beautification of cities was necessary, the planning of civic centers, malls and promenades did not, even then, answer the most compelling needs. It was a backward and formal gesture, and it served the interests of the leisure class. What Sullivan might have done instead is suggested by his later understanding of the concept of the garden city; and in these years it was suggested by his use of the setback in the design for the Fraternity Temple and by what he felt was the harmony of mass and ornament in the Wainwright Building.

Sullivan rehearsed the course of thought and experiment that led to the Wainwright Building in a paper on "Ornament in Architecture." From Richardson he had learned that without ornament mass and proportion might convey a noble sentiment; and he had returned, first in the Dexter Building and then in the Walker Warehouse, to simple and naked forms. But he had also learned from Whitman that his yearning for expression was good—and manly, that it was the impulse of life in the artist, and that its architectural expression might imbue a building with life. Art, after all, was emotional expression; it grew out of the nature of man and answered more than utilitarian needs. The emotional appeal of mass and proportion, he believed, was more profound, the appeal of ornament more intense. Both, however, sprang from the same source of feeling, and together they made architecture a noble eloquence.

For Sullivan, the building—not just its ornament—was, as Whitman said of his leaves, the herbage of his breast. Ornament and structure were integral; their subtle rhythm sustained a high emotional tension yet produced a sense of serenity. (His analogy was music.) But the building's identity resided in the ornament. It was the spirit animating the mass and flowing from it, and it expressed the individuality of the building. Nurtured by the artist's sympathy with life, the ornament spoke: it was the voice of the artist and of the building—indeed, they were one, the building a "stock-personality," and its architect an interpreter and prophet.

Such spiritual results, Sullivan insisted, could only be achieved in America—"the garden of our world." Here, he said, "tradition is without shackles, and the soul of man free to grow, to mature, to seek its own." Thus, when he began again to ornament his buildings—and the system of ornamentation was no longer derivative, but uniquely his own—he hoped that the ornament would teach this lesson. "We shall learn," he said, "to consider man and his ways, to the end that we behold the unfolding of the soul in all its beauty. . . ."[25] Ornament spoke with the inspiration of Ocean Springs.

And because of this inspiration the paramount problem of the Wainwright Building was the transcendence of the "sinister" urban conditions that necessitated tall buildings. Sullivan asked the question that Whitman had asked of materialistic America in *Democratic Vistas:* "How shall we impart to this sterile pile, this crude, harsh, brutal agglomeration, this stark, staring exclamation of eternal strife, the graciousness of . . . higher forms of sensibility and culture . . . ?" This problem accounts for Sullivan's feeling that the tall office building was "one of the

The Wainwright Building (1890-91)

Buildings that soar

The Getty Tomb (1890)

Whispers of Heavenly Death

most stupendous, one of the most magnificient opportunities . . . ever offered to the proud spirit of man." Accepting the social conditions as an inevitable part of the problem to be solved, Sullivan made the Wainwright Building an example of the transformation of utility into beauty. This soaring skyscraper was his affirmation of the proud spirit of man, his form against Fate.[26] And only an architect so aware and so inspired could have built, at the same time, the Wainwright and Getty Tombs—those poems, worthy of Whitman's, to "heavenly death."

Fashioned of lath and staff, the classic buildings of the World's Columbian Exposition did not endure as long as the idea they represented. Recapitulating the scenes of Thomas Cole's *The Course of Empire*, they arose on the swampy waste of Jackson Park—a veritable *Consummation*. But when they were razed their effigy in stone appeared everywhere. And Daniel Burnham, who supervised the construction of the Fair, proved right: "The influence of the Exposition on architecture will be to inspire a reversion toward the pure ideal of the ancients. We have been in an inventive period, and have had rather contempt for the classics. Men evolved new ideas and imagined they could start a new school without much reference to the past. But action and reaction are equal. . . . It will be unavailing hereafter to say that great classic forms are undesirable. The people have the vision before them . . . and words cannot efface it." [27]

The Chicago School did not die with the Fair. But it momentarily yielded to the architects from the East who represented the dominant taste of the time.[28] Never secure in its feeling of Western superiority, the Chicago School was not prepared to challenge the hegemony of the East. As early as 1886, Root, the Western Association's delegate, told the convention of the American Institute of Architects that the West was not in competition with them; and when he referred to the "Wild West" he perhaps admitted more than he intended.[29] The American Institute of Architects held its convention in Chicago in 1887; both associations consolidated in 1889. And from the beginning, the Westerners, who might have built the Fair themselves, were willing to make it a national undertaking. Unlike the Easterners, who, Henry Van Brunt said, were a "family . . . brought up under the same academical influences," they never had the certainty of an assured style.[30] When taste contested creative vitality, taste won. As Veblen, who appreciated the lesson of the Fair, said, "The office of the leisure class in social evolution is to retard the movement and to conserve what is obsolescent." [31] Sullivan, not having Veblen's gifts of detachment or irony, later spoke of the Fair as an incubus and contagion, a dark cloud blighting the land. Within his system of thought, the Fair represented the Rhythm of Death, and when he spoke of a thought in decadence producing a form in decadence, the Fair was ever in his mind.

The Fair, however, was not the final word in the argument over styles. The issue was never so conclusively settled, and the battle of styles continued because the underlying issue, as Sullivan knew, was that of the present against the past, of life against death. From Emerson's day to ours this larger battle has been fought anew in every generation. Considering the Fair, Walter Behrendt concluded that "the tragic fate of the United States [is] its inability to achieve spiritual continuity. . . ."[32] But if that continuity is not to be found in American architecture, it can be found in the attempt of every generation to discover the human meaning and possibility of America. That is why Sullivan turned hopefully to the young, and, why, in *Kindergarten Chats*, he defined American architecture in terms of the full realization of man. "The architecture *we* seek," he said, "shall be as a man active, alert, supple, strong, sane. A generative man. A man having five senses all awake; eyes that fully see, ears that are attuned to every sound; a man living in his present, knowing and feeling the vibrancy of that ever-moving moment, with heart to draw it in and mind to put it out: that incessant, that portentous birth, that fertile moment we call Today! As a man who knows his day, who loves his day, who knows and loves the exercise of life, who rightly values strength and kindliness, whose feet are on the earth, whose brain is keyed to the ceaseless song of his kind: who sees the past with kindly eye, who sees the future in a kindling vision: as a man who wills to create. So shall our art be. For to live, wholly to live, is the manifest consummation of existence." The spirit of Emerson, Thoreau, and Whitman—the quintessential spirit of America—had found another spokesman.

3: THE AMERICAN SCHOLAR

If, as I hold, true scholarship is of the highest use-fulness because it implies the possession and the application of the highest type of thought, imagination and sympathy, his work must so reflect his scholarship as to prove that it has drawn him toward his people, not away from them; that his scholarship has been used as a means toward attaining their end, hence his. That his scholarship has been applied for the good and the enlightenment of all the people, not for the pampering of a class. His works must prove, in short (and the burden of proof is on him), that he is a citizen, not a lackey, a true exponent of democracy not a tool of the most insidious form of anarchy . . . in a democracy there can be but one fundamental test of citizenship, namely: Are you using such gifts as you possess for or against the people?

                    Sullivan, Kindergarten Chats (1901-1902)

It was not the World's Fair, but the panic of 1893, the ensuing depression, Adler's withdrawal from the firm in 1895, and

Sullivan's own arrogance that altered the course of his career. Without Adler, the lean years were leaner, and the number of commissions diminished. Except for a few factories and small buildings, Sullivan completed only three major projects in the next decade: the Bayard Building in New York, the façade of the Gage Building and the Schlesinger & Mayer Department Store in Chicago. These were the ripe work of a mature artist, and they added to his fame.[1] In fact, though he built less he gathered more praise than ever before. If clients no longer turned to him, aspiring architects did, and by 1900 he was recognized as the leader of the new movement in architecture.

Even his address before the convention of the American Institute of Architects in New York in 1894, on "Emotional Architecture as Compared with Intellectual," which marked the beginning of a long battle over the education of the architect, did not hinder his election to the Institute's Board of Directors. He was a member of the Board from 1895-97, and served on the Executive Committee in 1895, when Daniel Burnham was president. The loyal McLean continued to back him in *The Inland Architect*: the honors France bestowed on him in 1895 for his work at the Fair were fully reported; everything he wrote, even minor editorials, was printed or reprinted; space was always available for the pictorial record of his work; his skyscrapers were praised; and in a second series on the question of styles ("Is Architecture a Living Art?") in 1897, he was upheld. From the time of the appearance of the critical articles of Barr Ferree in 1894 and Montgomery Schuyler in 1895, Sullivan's work was increasingly recognized and appreciated.

It was even defended. The unfailingly generous Adler, for example, expounded Sullivan's doctrine that form follows function before the convention of the American Institute of Architects in 1896. He restated and amplified the theory of Sullivan's article, "The Tall Office Building Artistically Considered," printed earlier that year in *Lippincott's,* definitely attributed the doctrine of functionalism to his former partner, and maintained, as Sullivan would have, that he was protesting against "the dogma that art in architecture ended with the Renaissance. . . . ." [2] In the next year, McLean praised Sullivan's skyscrapers. And even as late as 1905, when the tide of acclaim was ebbing, F. W. Fitzpatrick spoke of Sullivan as the first architect in Chicago to put aside precedent. "Speaking of the new school," he wrote, "I am thinking of Mr. Sullivan." [3]

Fitzpatrick was not thinking of the Chicago School but of another school that had grown up beside it. This school was composed almost entirely of young draftsmen who did not have the academic training or credentials needed for professional standing in the American Institute of Architects. The architectural clubs that began in the 1880's had been the nucleus. They had educated draftsmen, had drawn together the junior members of the profession, and, unlike the American Institute of Architects, had held annual exhibitions of architectural work. In time, both the membership and the program of the clubs had broadened. Never strictly professional, never maintaining the distinction between master and apprentice, they accepted artists and amateurs; and they turned to the problems represented by the emerging interest in arts and crafts, city improvement, and general art education. (Sullivan joined the Illinois Industrial Arts League, another organization interested in these problems, in 1899.) These independent clubs were organized as The Architectural League of America in 1899, and the League was immediately hailed as a new force in American architecture. Its officers were soon listed beneath those of the American Institute in *The Inland Architect*, which spoke of the organization of the League as "the most notable event in the architectural history of this country since the revival of the American Institute of Architects and its consolidation with the Western Association." And later, still hoping for the development of a national architecture, it turned to "this new school"—to "Sullivan and the young men who have followed his tracks. . . ." [4]

Much of the critical attention Sullivan received at this time was the result of his apotheosis by the League. He had not chosen to lead; instead, a new generation rekindling the aims of the Chicago School had chosen him as their spokesman. Max Dunning, the secretary of the Chicago Architectural Club (and Sullivan's most helpful supporter in his later years of decline), had inaugurated the League, and at its first convention in Cleveland in 1899, had read Sullivan's "The Modern Phase of Architecture." This paper, which was immediately printed in *The Inland Architect,* distinguished by a decorative border, and used to preface the report of the convention, was said to be "the event of the convention, so thoroughly did it embody the thought and feelings of every draftsman present. . . ." In it, Sullivan spoke of the formation of League as the auspicious opening of a new era; he placed the possibility of an American art in the hands of the younger generation—"I have said good-bye to mine [my youth]; with solicitude I welcome yours"; and briefly explaining his belief that the architect is the poet and interpreter of national life and allying himself with the new generation, he called upon the League, "not to betray, but to express the life of your own day and generation." [5] It was a ringing address, a reporter noted, and at the next convention was referred to as "the cornerstone of our organization." [6] The convention accepted Sullivan's challenge: it was made a part of the League's constitution—"To encourage an indigenous and inventive architecture, and to lead architectural thought to modern sources of inspiration."

The occasion of Sullivan's greatest triumph, however, was the second convention of the League, held in the Auditorium Hotel in 1900. Only a month before the convention, George R. Dean's article, "Progress before Precedent," had provided a slogan and the issue for debate.[7] Sullivan acknowledged this article, and it probably prompted the extremity of his attack on the present—the older, the established—generation of architects in his convention address, "The Young Man in Architecture." But even before this speech, delivered at the banquet closing the convention (the setting: the dining room he had designed; the toastmaster, his rival and the present generation incarnate: Daniel Burnham), his reception by the convention had been overwhelming.

In the debate on "Progress before Precedent," Sullivan had been moved by unexpected tribute. Introducing his paper on " 'Indigenous and Inventive Architecture' for America," Elmer Grey referred to "the man who, above all others, has stimulated us . . . by the most vital thought on architectural expression —Mr. Louis H. Sullivan." To this and the spirited applause, Sullivan responded by addressing the convention. He spoke extemporaneously for half an hour, extolling Grey's paper, which was close to his own thought, and developing his own ideas of inspiration in nature.[8] When the program resumed, Alexander Trowbridge of Cornell defended precedent. Alluding in passing to "Mr. Sullivan, to whom many turn in their search for originality," he hoped that "the schools will [not] drop precedent and organize on a Nature-study basis." [9] The next speaker, however, grandly supported Sullivan. Prefacing his paper on the discipline of nature, Frank Lloyd Wright remarked that "after listening to the master it hardly seem[s] proper to listen to the disciple. . . ." This open confession by the successful young man whom he had peremptorily dismissed from his office several years earlier for taking liberties with his contract undoubtedly warmed Sullivan more than the reception of his keynote speech. For when Wright described his own training, asserted that a "kindergarten circle of sympathetic discernment should be drawn about him [the architect] when he is born, and he should be brought into contact with Nature by prophet and seer until abiding sympathy with her is his," and spoke of the "encouraging guidance of a catholic-minded, Nature-wise, and loving master," he not only vindicated the man to whom he owed so much, but stirred within him the seed of *Kindergarten Chats*.[10] From this time on, Sullivan fully accepted the office of teacher, prophet, and seer.

That perhaps was the lasting value of his brief alliance with the League. Encouraged by *The Interstate Architect & Builder*, a minor weekly recently begun in Cleveland where the old Western enthusiasm had been revived by the League, Sullivan wrote out his program for architectural education. These *Kindergarten Chats*, which appeared in fifty-two installments from 1901 to 1902, were the special feature of the magazine, and they had been anticipated during the previous year by lavish editorial praise. "The Young Man in Architecture" had been printed with the editorial comment: ". . . the paper by Mr. Sullivan was a masterpiece in itself. Mr. Sullivan is not only a great architect, but a good writer as well." A month later, an editorial entitled "Without a Peer" claimed that "Louis H. Sullivan of Chicago is without question the most popular man in the profession in the United States" and that "the hard knocks Mr. Sullivan has been giving the moss-backed professors of architecture will certainly bring forth good fruit. . . ." Magazine space was allowed to those who wished to take issue, with the warning: "they may expect him to defend his position."

Two months before the first installment appeared, the magazine not only fulfilled its promise of a "rare treat" by publishing a ten-page pictorial review of Sullivan's work (presumably to be used as a standard for American architecture in the *Chats*),[11] but also published an "open" letter of Sullivan's which reflected his temper—and what sudden notoriety had done to him. In the letter, Sullivan charged the firm of Tenbusch & Hill with plagiarizing his designs. The letter, which was intemperate enough, might have been expected from the former chairman of the American Institute's committee on professional ethics, but it was followed by a tasteless double-page spread: on one page the design in question (one Sullivan had done for a swimming certificate for the Chicago Athletic Association!) was printed, on the facing page Tenbusch & Hill's design for the bronze door of the Cathedral of the Sacred Heart in Duluth. At the top of this page were printed the Standard Dictionary definitions of *plagiarism, unprincipled,* and *turpitude.* On the facing page appeared a photograph of Sullivan and a biographical note which mentioned his two years at the Beaux Arts and a style called "Sullivanesque."[12] Sullivan, who must have supplied these materials, had forgotten, in a moment of vainglory, what Dwight Perkins had said at the first convention of the League: "There is nothing whatever in his [Sullivan's] ideas that he does not believe any person, having poetic tendencies, cannot find expression for in building. He is not the only Sullivan."[13]

Perkins' statement about Sullivan's ideas was borne out by *Kindergarten Chats.* But the *Chats* were marred, at least superficially, by the same truculence Sullivan had exhibited in the denunciation of Tenbusch & Hill. Except for one letter from a reader, there was no response—the *Chats* were not even mentioned in *The Inland Architect* or in the reports of subsequent conventions of the League; and Sullivan's hope, that failing to be understood by architects, the *Chats* would be understood by the more open-minded public, came to nothing. What might have been the educational manual of the League and a genuine primer on architecture and society had for the most part gone unnoticed.[14] "I am amazed to note how insignificant . . . is the effect produced in comparison to the cost, in vitality, to me," he wrote Bragdon. "I shall never again make so great a sacrifice for the younger generation."[15]

Although Sullivan did not formally withdraw from the League, he did not attend the third convention—sending instead an encouraging letter.[16] But he attended the fourth convention in Toronto in 1902, at which he delivered his last address, "Education," a short coda on the *Chats.* At the fifth convention,

Claude Bragdon spoke of Sullivan's followers as standing "practically alone in the attempt to stem the rising tide of Latinism which floods the East and flows westward . . ." and he reminded the League that it was a living witness of Sullivan's influence.[17] But the League was no longer the power it had seemed to be only a few years before, when the president of the American Institute had suggested an alliance with it. Suffering the fate of many organizations, it became fixed in the routines of its exclusive concerns—the practical education of draftsmen and the preparations for the annual exhibition; and it was evident by the seventh convention in 1905 that its original impulse, which had promised so much, was spent. By this time Sullivan, apparently having lost the ready support of *The Inland Architect* and *The Interstate Architect,* had turned to *The Craftsman* for a wider audience and a new platform.[18]

After the Fair, the issue of styles was replaced by the question of a living architecture, and this question soon led to the more specific and relevant issue of education. Education, of course, had always been an important interest of the American Institute of Architects. The growth of the profession demanded stricter educational qualifications, and these were enforced by the increasing solidarity of the American Institute and the professional schools. After their victory at the Fair, the classicists, led by Charles McKim, established the American Academy in Rome; training at the Beaux Arts became popular and professors of architecture began to be more prominent in the journals. The restrictive tendency of this academic influence was responsible for the countervailing movement represented by the League. To Sullivan, who was aware of the larger educational revolution of the time and who clearly saw the relation between effete art and slavish adherence to tradition, the paramount object of attack was now the new academicism.

None of the critics of architectural education went as far as

Sullivan did when he addressed the American Institute in 1894. Frederick Baumann only restated the issue, that architecture in America had become a "dead art" and that the hope of a vital art depended on better educated students. He did not offer a discipline, but he proposed its end—that the architect become a teacher of the people; and he insisted, as he had in earlier discussions, that "style notions" be abandoned. For the most part, architects did not respond to this summons to leadership any more than they had to Sullivan's. They believed with Peter B. Wight (who replied to Baumann), that they were followers, not leaders of the people, and they preferred to listen to William R. Ware, Sullivan's first teacher, who claimed that the classic style was the best for present needs.[19] In this way the major point was reduced to a minor one; as the argument circled its various issues it was dissipated.

Thus Sullivan was forced to reiterate his demands for education in the most compelling terms. He had always been more concerned with the inspiration that determined style than with style itself, and his concern was always vigorously—and, in time, immoderately—expressed. Supported now by wider reading in educational theory and psychology, and perturbed more and more by his own wasted powers and his fears for democracy, he wrote a series of essays that rightly belong with *The American Scholar*. Like Emerson before him, he undermined the schools and the interests they sustained. He challenged the discipline of books and the training of the intellect and championed the discipline of nature and the development of the whole man. He placed his hope for the conversion of the world in the self-reliant and responsible man, and the goal of this conversion he called "democracy."

All the elements of Sullivan's thought appear clearly for the first time in his greatest address, "Emotional Architecture as Compared with Intellectual: A Study in Objective and Subjective." [20] This cogent essay redeemed the earlier rhapsody on "Inspiration," and challenged the classicists in their own stronghold. Sullivan did not, as in later addresses, directly attack historical styles or accuse the older generation of architects of betraying their trust and of reducing architecture to "zero." He spoke instead of education and explained why it was accountable for the present sterility in architectural art. His initial remarks were deceptively neutral, but the contrasting notions they contained, when skillfully developed, were not. "How strange it seems," he began, "that education, in practice, so often means suppression. . . ." Then, as if with tacit consent, he announced his own view: "Yet evidently the true object of education, now as ever, is to develop the capabilities of the head and of the heart."

Assuming that education was growth, Sullivan went on to describe, as he had done before and would do more fully in his books, the primary education of a simple youth in nature. He explained the notion of identity he had learned from Whitman, how the boy and natural objects "expand side by side, defining themselves intimately to each other"; and, more deeply versed in Whitman, he now stressed touch, "the exquisite touch of the sensibilities, the warm physical touch of the body . . . in spontaneous communion with Nature." The education he prescribed was initially of the senses; for him the transcendental faculty of intuition was an "exalted animal sense"—like the arch, it was only the furthest reach of the physical. He did not denigrate the intellect; instead he grounded it in the "perfect concrete analysis [of] the senses and the sympathies. . . ."

The education Sullivan proposed was, as Emerson had said, a genuine "*e-ducation* or calling out of [the] faculties." [21] Nature was the best of teachers, yet further growth depended on the student whose "yearning, ever unsatisfied," Sullivan said, was "the dominant characteristic of man's eminence in nature. . . ." (He noted, too, that it was "the justification of the eminence of a few men among their fellows.") For desire turned the student to the external world and compelled the singleness of purpose with which he selected the nourishment of his faculties. The child not only went forth and identified with things, but, led by desire—the very germ of the self—he chose those things that best fitted the needs of his developing self. That is why Sullivan attacked repressive theories of education and admonished architects as Emerson had his congregation: "O quench not his [the child's] hope, O do not repress one impulse of enthusiasm. . . ." [22] Both believed—it was as central to their thought as it was to the educational theories of Froebel and Dewey—in the idea of organic education and nurture Emerson had found in Sampson Reed's *Growth of the Mind*: "The mind must grow, not from external accretion, but from an internal principle. Much may be done by others in aid of its development; but in all that is done, it should not be forgotten, that, even from its earliest infancy, it possesses a character and a principle of freedom, which *should be* respected, and *cannot* be destroyed. Its peculiar propensities may be discerned, and proper nutriment and culture supplied; but the infant plant, not less than the aged tree, must be permitted, with its own organs of absorption, to separate that which is peculiarly adapted to itself; otherwise it will be cast off as a foreign substance, or produce nothing but rottenness and deformity." [23] The failure to heed this counsel and all it implies for culture and society, explained for both Emerson and Sullivan the sterility of their times.

Because of another desire—the desire to act—that which the mind assimilated became thought and expression. The mind, Emerson said, had a receptive and a constructive pole; its rhythm was one of influx and efflux. Sullivan spoke of "the desire to absorb and the desire to emit"; and as an artist, he, too, was concerned with the complete circuit of thought and with those agencies cr faculties that fulfilled the desire for expression or action. He called these agencies "imagination," "thought," and "expression."

Imagination, he explained, arises in the spontaneous response to the world of one's entire being. It is the agent of that "illumined instant" in which ideas are born, and it is primary because it alone is generative. To it Sullivan attributed all that Coleridge meant when he said that "the primary Imagination I hold to be the living power and prime agent of all human perception, and as a repetition in the finite mind of the eternal act of creation in the infinite I AM." Thinking of his own creative process, Sullivan noted that from the moment of perception all is "a foregone conclusion, an absolute certainty . . . a task surely, but not a doubt." Thought (comparable to Coleridge's The Understanding) is the analytical and critical faculty that makes the task easier. It serves by defining "the scheme and structure that is to underlie, penetrate, and support the form of an art work." An agent that "goes slowly, deliberately, that makes very firm and sure," it also is associated with constraint and the limitations of materials. "It is the hard, the bony structure," he remarked, ". . . never the smile." Expression is the smile. The office of this "winsome one, exuberant in life and movement, copious in speech" is to "clothe the structure . . . with a form of beauty. . . ." Expression restores the plasticity of life; she is an ornamentalist.[24]

These agencies are natural, and the creation they further is, like the development of man, a natural process of growth and elaboration. Such art is valuable because it reproduces human experience: "by a process of elaboration and growth, through the natural storage and upbuilding of the products of nutrition lifting themselves higher and higher into organization, the physical and spiritual experiences of our lives, seeking reproduction, find imaginative utterance, in their own image. . . ." The result of a unitary impulse (the agencies are not separated in act), such art has life—and style. For both the living quality of art and its style come from "the actual, vital first-hand experiences of the one who made it. . . ."

The architect does more than build: he communicates. His work is a metaphor and has the suggestive and fugitive qualities of metaphor. As Emerson said, a building is a spiritual form; it is not simply an organic form in the utilitarian sense, but is in itself constitutive of reality. Spiritual forms, accordingly, have life—the fluency of spirit—and they also have the ultimate qualities of spirit: equilibrium and repose. Even if one does not accept the transcendental notion of reality, the experience which such forms convey is still that of man's deepest and most intense interaction with nature. Sullivan, who like Emerson equated "inner" (the subjective) with "above" (the transcendental reality), spoke in religious terms of the first-hand experience that vitalized the self and thereby art. The foundation of art was "that extraordinary communion that the sacred writers called to 'walk with God.' "

This original relationship is bestowed by nature on the child who ever afterwards seeks to satisfy the "hunger for the spiritual" which is a condition of his development. That he fails—and that architecture is stillborn—is the result of repressive, one-sided education of the intellect. It is this "education's crime," Sullivan said, "that it has removed us from Nature."

In itself intellect is not the malefactor. As Sullivan had shown, it is an agent of creative thought. In his discourse, however, it is always associated with the objective. Objective and subjective, intellectual and emotional—these are phases of the rhythm of thought, and this rhythm in the life of man corresponds to the rhythm of decadence and growth in nature. Thus for Sullivan, intellect carries with it the implications of materialism and restraint—of rigidity. It also carries all the meanings ascribed to it by the romantics, who, like Sullivan, wished to end the strife of head and heart by dethroning the usurping head and by making the heart sovereign. Sullivan affirmed the necessity and primacy of the heart in his account of self-development and creativity.

Viewed historically, the intellect-dominant is feudalism. To attribute the failure of architecture to an education of the intellect is thus a way of calling that education feudal. It is also a way of calling architecture and education to judgment, for they can now be measured against the relentless democratic impulse Sullivan believed to be the vital force of history. His own time, he felt, was feudal, marked by "murky materialism," "fierce objectivity," and "fanatical selfishness"; he called it "this dark age of ours," and he placed his hope for the democratic dawn in a reaction to its excess. Like Whitman, Sullivan accepted materialism as the basis of the coming spiritual era; and, following Whitman, he opened a democratic vista by cataloging the events that had enacted and were enacting the democratic destiny. His catalog began with Hindu, Hebrew, and Chaldean in search of God; it included the objective Greek and the emotional Goth; it recognized the advent of modern science and the political and industrial revolutions still in progress; and it terminated in America—"a new land, a Promised Land. . . ." "*Here,*" Sullivan announced, "*destiny has decreed there shall be enacted the final part in the drama of man's emancipation—the redemption of his soul!*"

The poet of "Inspiration" had now become a prophet. But the grandeur of his prophecy, like that of prophets of old, was also a preparation for arraignment. Once more, with greater attention to detail, he denounced "the utterly purposeless education we have received." He eloquently questioned the "stewardship" of his generation of architects and recounted their excuses only to chasten them. And, finally, he summoned them to true leadership. The architect, he claimed, was the true exponent of his time; in his art he seeks "a natural expression of our lives, of our thoughts, of our meditations, our feelings. . . ." With the

The Guaranty Building (1894-95)

Mobile Equilibrium

proper education, he will have the *"manliness"* needed for his art. And his art will at last be a complete art, one of both head and heart. Truly plastic, responsive to the "fluctuations of man's inner being," the new art will unite the "statics" of the Greek and the "dynamics" of the Gothic. It will have the "mobile equilibrium" of nature and "shall speak with clearness, with eloquence, and with warmth, of the fullness, the completeness of man's intercourse with Nature and with his fellow men." It will be the issue of the freely developing man, and it will be an architecture of democracy.

Sullivan provided the object lesson demanded by this address in his next and most widely published paper, "The Tall Office Building Artistically Considered." [25] His text might have been Whitman's statement: "The direct trial of him who would be the greatest poet is today." [26] For he wanted to show how, in answer to current needs and without consulting books, he would build a "true, normal type"—one, moreover, that transcended feudal conditions by expressing the democratic aspirations of man. To this end he enunciated the doctrine that form follows function and exemplified the corollary: that every problem contains and suggests its own solution. He discussed the social conditions that made tall buildings necessary; he explained the physiology of the building and its honest exterior treatment; then he spoke of architectural expression and the eloquence of "loftiness." (For Sullivan, expression, the subjective element, is inevitably democratic. The essay moves from objective to subjective considerations.) He considered the theories that might be applied to the tall building: that it was a classic column, with base, shaft, and capital; that it was the mystical trinity; that it was a logical statement, with a beginning, middle, and end; that it was organic, like leaves, stem, and flower, or a pine tree (here, as in his remarks on the internal lighting court, he anticipated Frank Lloyd Wright). But all these *a priori* solutions he rejected. The identity of a building was not to be imposed but discovered and expressed. Form follows function was a rule of discovery and expression, and its implications would have been more clearly recognized if it had been stated: function creates form. For Sullivan had learned from nature, not to use the pine-tree as a model, but rather to search out and follow the process by which the tree achieves its identity. Functions *seek* their forms: "life seeks and takes on its forms in an accord perfectly responsive to its needs. It seems ever as though the life and the form were absolutely one and inseparable so adequate is the sense of fulfillment." The architect, therefore, studies need—not books. If the building he described (either the Wainwright or the Guaranty Building) had a three-part division, this, he claimed, was not the result of theory but the natural and spontaneous result of its functions. Designed in this way, the tall office building was a new architectural type. Designed by an architect with a "sense of responsibility to the generation he lives in," it might even be the living architecture "of the people, for the people, and by the people."

These essays contained all that Sullivan preached when he became the mentor of the League. Only the accent changed, sharpened by adulation and support: he now spoke out as a partisan. The line of battle was distinctly drawn: the older generation in adhering to styles had betrayed its trust; failing to nurture the powers of man and to supply the discipline of "natural thinking," its schools had contributed to the spiritual impotence of democracy. Providing instead a "mental nourishment at the withered breast of Despotism," the schools perpetuated a "reactionary education," and this, he maintained, accounted for the "frightful waste" of talent. Properly trained, that talent would serve the public welfare.

In "The Young Man in Architecture," Sullivan tried to weld the dissidents together by insisting that "no aid is to be expected from the generation now representing that malpractice. . . ." [27] He exploited and intensified the discontent in order to glorify the hope with which he charged the new generation. He ridiculed: "American architecture," he asserted, "is . . . ninety parts aberration, eight parts indifference, one part poverty and one part Little Lord Fauntleroy. You can have the prescription filled at any architectural department-store, or select architectural millinery establishment." He reduced the intellectual allegiances of architects to "cacophony": "The purring of the select company of Ruskinites," "The gasping of the Emersonites" (Emerson had been claimed by the genteel), "The rasping of the Spencerites" (In *Kindergarten Chats* he said, "Nature favors the apt, not the strong. . . ."), "The moaning of the Tennysonites." He called their work perverse, for they used the "steel frame function in a masonry form"—a grotesquerie best realized by imagining "Horse-eagles" or "Tarantula-potatoes." Every article of his own creed anathematized theirs: to begin an architect's education with a book, he said, would be an "intellectual crime."

Sullivan told the young men of the new generation that they would have to educate themselves. They would have to begin by observing nature and by learning the lesson of her "spontaneous logic." Equally important, they would have to become students of psychology, for "the human mind," Sullivan said, "is the original document." [28] In the practice of their art, they would have to return to the basic elements, to the pier, the lintel, and the arch, and the desire within their hearts. And to build for democracy they would have to accept not only the impulse to freedom which is its essence, but the decision to use it wisely and beneficently which is its duty. He concluded by stressing responsibility and choice: "Do you intend or do you not intend . . . to become architects in whose care an unfolding Democracy may entrust the interpretation of its material wants, its psychic aspirations?" He might have added, as Emerson had in a similar address to young men, "the hour of that choice is the crisis of your history. . . ." [29]

"I am not tolerant of that aristocratic spirit which mis-directs American youth in its search for knowledge—and would seek to impose upon it those formulas of learning and attitudes of mind toward learning which have descended to us from times when education was for the 'gentleman'—for the few, for a class: that 'education' which separates one from his people by the violence of its badge of alienation and uselessness." The teacher is speaking to the student of *Kindergarten Chats*.[30] He explains that this is what the schools of architecture of the day are doing, and that they are actively pernicious because they do not train the young to deal with the realities of American life. Their professors are "pettifoggers of the Middle Ages"; tradition and custom have shut them out from the world's activities—they are the victims of trained incapacity. The teacher shares Veblen's views of higher education. In other fields, however, he finds that education has advanced because it has been based on a new psychology and metaphysics: ". . . the *kindergarten* has brought bloom to the mind of many a child: and . . . this is the result of a growing philosophy of education." He regrets that there is no architectural kindergarten—"a garden of the heart wherein the simple, obvious truths, the truths that any child might consent to, are brought fresh to the faculties and are held to be good because they are true and real." The student, who rather patiently takes the brunt of these re-marks, thinks them uncalled for. He accuses the teacher of striking at the root of what he has been brought up to revere; and when the teacher continues to attack the schools, his only defense is to ask, "What should be done about it?" The teacher replies, "What I am doing to you."

The student of the *Chats* is not a member of the League. He is a graduate of a school of architecture, and his attitudes are representative of those of the American Institute of Architects. The teacher mocks his qualifications: "You are precisely the young, 'well-educated,' self-confident and unsuspecting hopeful I assumed you to be. . . ." The student has received the conventional college and fine-art education of the day; "you were not taught to observe what was going on in the great world . . . your school was engulfed and sealed up tight . . . your own mind was carefully and hermetically closed by your so-called teachers, after they had put into it whatever product of the past they thought it should contain." When the student fails to understand the teacher's explanations, the teacher reminds him of his superficial and slipshod education, how it handicaps him, how his knowledge is an "obnoxious minus quantity." He even tells him that it is his misfortune to have been city-bred, for "realities are images very difficult to awaken in a mind nurtured in an atmosphere of unreality and falsehood." It is also his misfortune to have been raised in the East, "cradled in the culture of older and wiser parts of our land. . . ."

Why the student follows the teacher is a mystery the *Chats* never explains. In actuality, few students did. Most, if they read the *Chats* at all, must have felt as the student does in a moment of revulsion: "You are running counter to your day and generation and to mine. You seek to impose your will: to substitute your vision—to create an apocalypse for a heedless world. . . . Why should I differ from my day and generation? No one will pay me any Dollars for being a seer and a prophet." But it was perhaps enough for the purposes of the *Chats* that the student represented youth. For having youth, having spirit, is his salvation. He may have received his former education ("like any other sample of canned goods"), but now, confronted by a teacher whose taunts are methodological, he responds and participates in his own education. He soon becomes argumentative, then irritable, finally critical. In time, he learns the teacher's doctrine through experience; he begins to express himself and is reborn—not only as an architect but as a man. His education is difficult and perhaps brutal because it is reeducation. What the teacher wants to change are, in Veblen's phrase, habits of thought. His intention is Whitman's:

Stop this day and night with me and you shall possess the origin of all poems,
You shall possess the good of the earth and sun . . .
You shall no longer take things at second or third hand, nor look through the eyes of the dead, nor feed on the spectres in books,
You shall not look through my eyes either, nor take things from me,
You shall listen to all sides and filter them from your self.[31]

If the teacher's method appears brutal—some have dismissed the *Chats* because they found it so—its brutality is in the service of love. The teacher explains that his wrath is not directed at the student but at the schools and that the student, whom he loves, stands "for all the youth of our land." In fact the teacher is motivated, as he said are the teachers of the kindergarten, by enthusiasm, love, and devotion. He tells the student that he does not seek to instruct or reconstruct him. "I shall seek, only," he explains in his first example of organic growth, "to persuade the faculties which nature gave you at birth, and which, now, are partly shriveled, to revivify, to send out new roots, to grow, to expand, and to bring forth as nature intended." To this end, he provides the most expensive kind of education.

For the education is an experience, an active confrontation of student and teacher; it is personal and direct—a dialogue initiated by the observation and experience of things. The teacher, even more than the student, unstintingly bestows himself. He accepts the responsibility he asks the architect to accept: he nurtures life. "You are for me," the teacher says, "the neglected but fallow field, under the broad sky of humanity: to be plowed, to turn under the weeds and bring up the subsoil; and then, harrowed for a while, to give it tilth. I will plant therein the seeds of many thoughts; but they must germinate in the fertile darkness of your own soul, under the beneficent influence of the compelling sun that shines for all. . . . But I will also be the good gardener. And, when these tiny seeds put forth into the light their tender shoots and leaves, each after its kind, I will care for them, and water them with the water of life, drawn from nature's well-spring. Thus shall you grow, and put forth branch and bud. The fragrance of your blooming shall be my reward; the fruit thereof shall be yours." This is one of the great avowals of dedication to education. One is reminded of Alcott—and also of Woolson—and of Froebel who said that the kindergarten is the garden of children and the teacher the children's gardener. When the teacher expatiates on human growth in "The Tulip," the student remarks that he should have been a gardener of men. Indeed, by recovering the student's fertile childhood he hopes to become one. Culture, for him, is literally nurture; and its end, in nature and man, is the fulfillment of "normal and complete desire."

There is nothing recondite in this education. It has many antecedents, but Sullivan based it on Whitman and on the new psychology and pedagogy Dewey was experimenting with in the Elementary School recently begun at the University of Chicago.[32] It is education out-of-doors—in the real world; there are no books—the objects are real, known in present experience. In activity and play, the vital response of sensation and perception educates the faculties, not separately but in ensemble. The responses of teacher and student differ and give rise to new awareness. Even when, at last, they share the same vision, the student and teacher sing separate parts of their chorale to spring. Dialogue, of course, permitted Sullivan to represent himself in both youth and age and to be true to his own doubts and despair, but it was used also because it enacted his belief in the freedom to question. The teacher is a personal, sympathetic guide, and each episode is a demonstration for which his "I think" makes him responsible.

Finally, this education is dialectical. Its logic follows that of organic growth. The growth of the student from within, his enthusiasms, pessimism, and hope, is made to correspond with the seasons; and as season follows season, he grows and ripens. This drama of growth is also intensified by suggestions of a spiritual journey. The seasons, though cyclical, provide the dialectic of the upward way. The teacher, who at various times wears the mantles of Whitman, Zarathustra, Vergil, and Moses, leads the student from valley to summit, from Dis to nature, from Egypt to the promised land: "I will give you the landmarks and the blazings in that country which I have explored alone: but it is the land of promise—and I return to tell you of it, and to point the way." (Moses, here, is an American pioneer.) After the student's awakening, the teacher suggests that they "climb the summit somewhat higher," and he does not leave the student until he has lived through the rhythm of growth and decay and has found in the returning glory of spring the permanent spring of hope.

The student's education begins with architecture. "I am going to soak you with it," the teacher warns him, "until you are nauseated. . . . When I am through with you, you will know architecture from the ground up." But the teacher, even here, is more concerned with training the sensibility and character of the youth who will one day act in society as an architect. Viewing buildings may have provided Sullivan with welcome occasions for criticizing contemporary architecture—he was a master of the rhetoric of denunciation, and enjoyed using it. But from the start, he was not criticizing buildings but builders, who were easily identified, and the irresponsibility of society at large; and he was suggesting, for he worked by indirection, the notion of form and function. This notion was both his critical tool and the summation of his philosophy. It was at the center of his theories of education, architecture, and democracy.

Forms—acts, words, stones, institutions—express functions, for function is a "pressure" or force that must be expressed; even its suppression tells. Forms are objective, the external manifestation of inner or subjective needs. The inevitability of their relation is conveyed in the dictum, form *follows* function. The critic does not describe forms so much as ask what functions they serve or express—or deny. In this way, he breaks through their masks. And to have learned to do this with buildings is simply a means of learning a lesson applicable to everything; whether in architecture or nature, the critic searches for the inner impulse, life, or spirit. "Folks," Whitman said, "expect of the poet to indicate more than the beauty and dignity which always attach to dumb real objects . . . they expect him to indicate the path between reality and their souls." [33] The path begins in sensation and ends in perception, that miraculous power of the mind. The see-er or seer is simply the perceiver: he sees the function in the form.

This is the path along which the teacher leads the student. He begins with the objective, with actual buildings. In the early episodes, he points out and ridicules various representative buildings (he never considers houses or the interiors of buildings): a building with a tower is "an ill-compounded salad, with a rather rancid New-Yorky flavor"; a terminal station is in "the public-be-damned style"; a department store seems to be a hotel and is called a "Judas"; a bank masquerades as a Roman temple; etc. These buildings are object lessons, and the title of the second chapter—"Pathology"—suggests their lesson. They raise the question that encloses the *Chats,* the question of national health; for they are indications of a "virus that is threatening our social life. . . ." They not only make the student aware of hidden causes, they also raise the further question of responsibility.

Both questions are answered in a general sociological way when the teacher explains what he had learned from Taine. Every building has a story to tell—the story of the man who made it and of the society which he reflects. The study of architecture is the study of the social conditions producing it and is therefore an index of tendencies within a civilization. The teacher insists that the student go behind the façade of things, that he consider the responsibility of builder and society. When the teacher ridicules the department store that looks like a hotel, the student not only is given an inkling of the relation of structure and purpose, he is forced to ponder the question of honesty; and when the teacher speaks of buildings as neuter or as having the qualities of femininity and manliness, he is confronted with "subjectivity" —with all that Sullivan meant by expression. In every instance he is taught to recognize that the inner determines the outer; he learns the *moral* symbolism of things.[34] The teacher tells him that "we will . . . trace physical appearances to their moral causes, and moral and social impulses to their manifestations in brick and stone." The gist of his teaching is given by Nietzsche: ". . . when [Zarathustra] saw a row of new houses, he marvelled, and said: 'What do these houses mean? Verily, no great soul put them up as its simile!' "[35] Thus the path from outer to inner ascends. What begins on the sociological level of "prudence"—to use Emerson's distinctions—mounts to the level of "spirit"; and this is as it should be, because for both Emerson and Sullivan material forms are the issue of spirit. Imperceptibly, the teacher becomes a philosopher.

The teacher's philosophy, as Emerson said of his, is a metaphysics to the end of use. The metaphysics is transcendental, its use is social. In the *Chats* the teacher most fully develops the metaphysics of form and function. The "Function of all functions," he finally explains, "is the Infinite Creative Spirit." The world, the rhythms of growth and decay, everything that comes into being and ceases to be in this process without beginning or end, is a manifestation of spirit, its form. As Emerson said in *Nature*, spirit "is that for which all things exist, and that by which they are . . . spirit creates. . . ."[36] Function and form —the play of creative impulse—is the law of life; and only when the student learns this lesson will he truly know the extent of his responsibility for his own creative powers. Thus, when the buildings have provided their elementary lessons, the teacher, once again abandoning precept for experience, takes the student directly to nature.

Nature's lesson is one of spirit—spirit both powerful and beneficent. The teacher has suggested relationships between the immaterial and the material, between the subjective and the objective; but now the student learns that these relationships indicate still another deeper one between the Infinite Spirit and the finite mind. His experience in nature stirs his suppressed creative impulse; he feels within him the surge of psychic power and realizes that he is not bound by the apparently deterministic chain of Taine's sociology. By sharing the powers of spirit he feels that he may become, as Emerson said, a "creator in the finite."[37] He begins to understand what the teacher had told him when speaking of the imagination, that nature is "fluent," the continuity of all that surrounds him, and that it is within him as well as without him—his "other self." Awakened by this revelation and overcome by his sense of being, the student feels that he is Adam in a new world. If, in an attempt to express himself, he soon finds that he is not yet disciplined enough to use his powers, it is sufficient for this stage of his education that he is alive to creative possibility.[38] He has learned for himself what the teacher later says is his real thesis—"that within man, a spiritual being, resides a spiritual power capable of infinite unfolding."

The teacher's thesis explains why he places all his hope for reform in education and why he is fervently committed to democracy. Spirit works in individual men, but its most fully realized social form is democracy. Democratic society, as the teacher defines it, is the form for this function and is created by the manifold relationships of individual men. It is felt in the forms they make. It is lived in—the total human environment which educates men. It is living when there is creation, when men do not deny but communicate their creative impulses and use them to nurture each other. The teacher's doctrine begins and ends in creation; it is a gospel of life whose measure is the fullness of life. At the heart of the doctrine of form and function is the impulse to life—an impulse to express life; and the doctrine is moral because in its uses it prescribes a rule of life. The deepest social meaning of the buildings the teacher ridicules is that, by suppressing function, they "deny life cautiously." And they are but one indication for him of the disease of genteel society, of the fact that "we have no present . . . except in a materialistic sense," that "in any other sense we seem empty and amorphous—without form and void. . . ."

Such criticism is an example of what Sullivan meant when he wrote Lyndon Smith that he was testing architecture by human nature and democracy.[39] He believed that the common enterprise of all men was to create value, to make "subjective what was before objective." Every form was to be shaped in the interests of life; the environment was to become fittingly human. This was the responsibility of the creator in the finite. And this is the responsibility the teacher expects the student to fulfill. He must not only be an architect, he must be the interpreter of the impulse of life that is latent in the people. He must be everything that Emerson meant by "American Scholar" and that Whitman meant by "Literatus."

As in Emerson and Whitman, this responsibility is based on a reassessment of man's powers and on his character. Man has the power to manipulate and overcome obstacles (Dewey), the power of mind or curiosity which implements his physical power (Dewey and Veblen), the power of his emotions which makes him a poet, the power of vision and dream which make him a prophet and interpreter, the power of spirit which helps him diffuse and concentrate his power, and the power of moral choice. All of these powers make man a creator, but the teacher emphasizes those that have been neglected by educators: the power of the emotions, of vision, of spirit, and of moral choice. He wishes to broaden the student's sympathies and to release the altruistic impulse which he believes is the normal impulse of the heart. The democratic education the teacher insists on should unfold all these powers and be psychologically liberating, thereby removing the causes of fear and resentment—those breeders of feudal malevolence. It must also, by laying bare the aims and workings of society, exercise his powers of choice. And it must, from the beginning, educate his character.

The teacher does this by directing the criticism of buildings to the men and society responsible for them. He deflates the popular notion of eminence by showing that the eminent do not have the necessary "moral altitude." He also distinguishes between "architek" and "architect," between the unimaginative and the imaginative. Everything he says throughout the *Chats* is intended to establish his vocation on the rock of character, to define a vocation he can justify. The student, however, does not immediately accept the large responsibilities with which the teacher tasks him. Not only has he misgivings about the teacher's open philosophy ("a philosophy which has no bottom and no top, no sides and no ends"), he also has misgivings about democracy. "*A bas* Democracy!" he says, mixing Carlyle and Lowell. "It is the refuge of the common, the average, the vulgar. Democracy eats with its knife. Do you mean to tell me a man can be a real man in a Democracy? A Dollar-man, yes! A cheap Dollar-man, cheap among the cheap. Look at them: all cheap, the richer the cheaper. Look at the faces: . . . all sordid, all pig-eyed, all self-centered in their democratic savagery. . . ." He believes with the Social Darwinists that men are not equal, that nature despises the weak and exalts the strong, and that the remedy for the disease of democracy is the autocratic leader. The herd do not seek freedom; they wish to be governed, and they need a "man big enough and strong enough and willful enough to guide and to govern." They care nothing for the genius, whom they "rend," nor for beneficent power; they respect force. Why, then, the student asks, should he be *"fined* for being a *real* architect . . . ?"

The teacher feels the force of these remarks. They represent common attitudes of the day, attitudes shaped by the education he attacks, and they measure the extent of his work. The student's revulsion is a necessary phase of growth, and the teacher allows him to express it. He does not immediately answer the student, but as the *Chats* go on, the foundations of the old attitudes are replaced with new views of nature, man, society, scholarship, and culture. They conclude by focusing all on the Representative Man, the architect (or intellectual) who accepts his role as citizen. For the Representative Man acknowledges his debt to the people who have nurtured his powers by using them to express their aspirations. To interpret the people to themselves, to outline the "courageous, creative and beneficent," and to initiate—these are his responsibilities and the tests of his eminence.

Kindergarten Chats (in the revised version of 1918, which incorporated the essential ideas of his later and unpublished book, *Democracy: A Man-Search*) is the most complete and forceful expression of Sullivan's thought. It is a singular book that has never accomplished its purpose; the misfortunes of out-of-the-way and delayed publication and its narrow identification with the field of architecture have contributed to its neglect. It deserves a more prominent place in the literature of democracy because it is the only book that shows the confluence of architectural thought with the broader intellectual currents of the time, and because in its concern for education, for the social responsibility of the intellectual, and for the realizable utopianism of democratic culture, it gathers up the rich tradition that preceded it and bestows it on our own age.

If Sullivan wrote it belligerently, it was because he felt that the very existence of democracy was at stake. Those who best represented the ideas he opposed—Irving Babbitt for example—were equally concerned and belligerent. It was not Babbitt but Robert S. Peabody, President of the American Institute of Architects, who said in response to Sullivan's ideas what Babbitt certainly would have, that "most of us shudder to think what our land would be if subjected to 'a liberation of the creative impulse.' " [40] Here was the crucial issue with which both Babbitt and Sullivan threaded their thought. Both, for different reasons, believed in the individual and in his power of moral choice—in this, neither succumbed to the prevailing social determinism. But they differed in their psychologies, in their views of nature, and thus in their willingness to liberate impulse. Both wrote histories (Babbitt, *Rousseau and Romanticism*; Sullivan, *Democracy: A Man-Search*) in which the protagonists were the ideas of restraint and freedom, the will to refrain and the will to liberate—and each chose the other's deity for his devil.

But the issue between them was not a simple one to be decided by temperament—though temperament will always have its say when freedom and restraint are in question. One must ask: freedom and restraint for what? For it is possible, as Sullivan recognized when he demanded responsibility, to invoke restraint in behalf of life. Restraint, as a general moral principle and as a superior imperative, is another matter—one that Sullivan explored in his search for the psychological causes of man's history. Creative impulse is not necessarily wanton, as the party of restraint supposed. Having known both restraint and freedom in his own experience (it was one of the themes of the *Autobiography*) and having found a warrant for freedom in the new thought of the age, which his detractors usually overlooked or impugned, Sullivan became an exponent of creative impulse. The guidance of life was not to be confused with the denial of life. That distinction was, for him, the real issue of the debate over education. To confuse this issue, as he believed man had often done in the course of history, was to forfeit democracy.

4: DEMOCRATIC VISTAS

The United States are destined either to surmount the gorgeous history of feudalism, or else prove the most tremendous failure of time.
Whitman, Democratic Vistas (1871)

It is pleasant to see before others what is coming, but it is hard to wait until enough of the others see it to make the coming possible.
Henry D. Lloyd, Man, The Social Creator (1906)

Economics was not as important in Sullivan's thought as it was in the thought of others whose general views on society he shared. But economics (and economies) was a considerable factor in the decline of his architectural fortunes, and had he been Veblen he might have analyzed the new architectural "plan factories" that made it difficult for him to survive in the competition for commissions. For nearly twenty years Sullivan's offices atop the Auditorium Tower had proclaimed his eminence, but a gradual decline in the number and size of commissions finally forced him to abandon them in 1909 for smaller rooms below. This professional comedown was probably the hardest, for he had already given up in a series of retrenchments whatever leisure class pretentions he had. As early as 1901 he had begun the movement to less expensive apartment-hotels that ended in 1911 with the rundown Warner Hotel on Cottage Grove Avenue and 33rd Street. His wife, Margaret Hattabough, whom he had married in 1899, left him in 1907, having taught him (one gathers from his letters to the caretaker at Ocean Springs) as much about the conspicuous needs of the leisure class as Veblen had. The panic of 1907 completed what the panic of 1893 began: in 1908, he gave up the cottage at Ocean Springs; he auctioned his library, art objects, and household effects in 1909, and resigned from the Chicago Club in 1910.

This is part of the dreary chronicle of decline he spared himself in the *Autobiography* (for example, he claimed that the cottage at Ocean Springs was wrecked by a hurricane), a chronicle which he might have made, had he wished, as socially significant as Dreiser's portrayal of Hurstwood's downfall in *Sister Carrie*. But Sullivan did not believe in Social Darwinism or economic determinism. If his failure had any significance, it was to be read in the broader "economic" terms of social value —in terms of waste. As an architect, his gifts had not been used; as a writer he felt that he had gone unheard. In "Education" (1902), he acknowledged this. "A democracy should not let its dreamers perish," he said. "They are its life, its guaranty against decay." He attributed his condition to neglect rather than to personal failure, and for this he blamed the "inverted thinking" of feudalism which he believed was the cause of both the sinister socioeconomic conditions and the architectual betrayal of the day.

In the *Autobiography* Sullivan noted in passing that in the glow and fury of early success he had not been socially aware. But each crisis deepened his awareness and widened the rift he perceived between feudalism and democracy. Though he always related architecture and society, in his first papers he had concentrated on the architectural aspects of the "characteristics and tendencies" of American life. He was concerned, naturally enough, with his own artistic development, with problems of inspiration and style. Now—having achieved a personal style and utterance only to find himself isolated by the very tendencies he had tried to overcome in his art—he became a forthright educator and social critic, impelled by a sense of urgency and an animus toward the survivals from the past that impeded reform. Architecture as it was generally practiced, he now realized, was but one survival. In criticizing it, he did for architecture what Dewey and Veblen, for example, were doing for education and economics: he reestablished its connection with a living and changing society. "To discuss architecture and ignore life is frivolous," he said in a statement typical of both his and the general critical temper of the time. And he added, pointing out the direction his inquiry had taken, that "to discuss American architecture and its possibilities, while ignoring the repressive force of feudalism and the expansive force of democracy, is sheer lunacy." [1] His writings now reflected this larger social concern—even their titles suggest it: "Natural Thinking: A Study in Democracy," "What is Architecture: A Study in the American People of Today," *Democracy: A Man-Search*. Still hoping for an American architecture, he enlisted his writings in the battle for democracy; he believed with Whitman that the doctrines of democracy "will only be effectually incarnated in any one branch, when, in all, their spirit is at the root and center." [2]

In one form or another feudalism and democracy had always been the poles of Sullivan's thought. They lurked in the comparisons of the educational worth of the schools and of nature and in the debates on styles and expression. The cultural nationalists had located them in space and time by contrasting the retrospective genteel culture of the East with the progressive masculine cultural possibilities of the West; and Frederick Jackson Turner, in an address at the World's Fair, had again made them relevant by showing how much these possibilities were threatened by the closing of the frontier. Whitman, of course, had given the terms currency in *Democratic Vistas,* and many writers, such as Twain and Adams, had weighed their values. W. J. Ghent called his popular survey of society, *Our Benevolent Feudalism* (1902), and Edward Carpenter, an English socialist whose Whitmanian gospel many professors at the University of Chicago embraced, called his complete poems, *Towards Democracy* (1905). As these books suggest, the terms had become charged with new significance—filled with the fears and hopes of a generation caught up in the rapid transformations of industrialism. The obsessiveness with which Sullivan now used them and the prophecies with which they inspired him were common; and, in his case, they indicated not a shallow moralism but the depth of his social concern. They were the heavy weapons of one who wished to batter down the doors that imprisoned life.

One measure of this concern was Sullivan's irritability when *The Craftsman* reopened the futile debate over styles in 1905. The debate, having kept pace with eclecticism, was now over the Gothic. Frederick Stymetz Lamb had invited discussion in an article in which he linked the Gothic with L'Art Nouveau and proposed the Gothic as a possible direction for architectural development. Following his lead, Professor A. D. F. Hamlin noted that "the truly Gothic procedure is best illustrated . . . in such office buildings as have been designed by Mr. Sullivan and Mr. Burnham. These are . . . the best examples of a real 'Art Nouveau' applied to architecture to be found anywhere to-day." [3] But Sullivan was not to be categorized in this fashion, neither associated with Burnham nor, by the implication of another paper, with the romanticism of Bertram Goodhue. He had always repudiated styles. And even before these later papers had been printed and before Lamb closed the debate with a statement whose irony Sullivan alone probably appreciated ("No-where in history can we find conditions which resemble our own as those existing during the Middle Ages") he had replied— and with the asperity of a preacher whose admonitions had not been heeded. In fact, all of his contributions to *The Craftsman* had a similar edge. For, as he reminded his readers, his solutions for the problems of American architecture were not new. "I have been preaching [them]," he said in one of his last papers in *The Craftsman*, "for twenty-five years." [4]

But he had never done so with such full awareness of impend-ing social crisis. The real problem, he wrote in his reply to Lamb, did not concern styles but "*us* here and now . . . the big urge of American life. . . ." Why, he asked, did architects fail to distinguish *was* and *is* and persist in the "ever-futile attempt to detach an art from the civilization which gave it birth?" Lamb seemed to assume that the objective forms of the past—the sur-vivals—were still alive; and "he complacently suggests," Sullivan sarcastically added, "that Mediaeval thought is really more Amer-ican than the thought of Greece or Rome—meanwhile com-pletely ignoring the possible suitability of twentieth century thought for our twentieth century conditions and demands."

Twentieth century thought for twentieth century conditions required the involvement with the present that was the very basis of "natural thinking"; and this was Sullivan's remedy for the inverted or artificial thinking and the "fetishism" of the past which were forever raising the spectres of styles. Styles, as he treated them now, were merely a sign of the general nightmare from which he hoped to awaken America; a nightmare he ex-plained by briefly and vividly recounting the history of America from its pristine beginnings and opportunities to its present state of degradation. His history was natural history, a story of growth (organization) and decay (disintegration) in which the forces of life were losing: "So rapidly, thoughtlessly and loosely did they organize and prosper, that disintegration (as was inevitable) kept a gaining-pace within their minds and their social structure, and, hence, corruption steadily worked an ascendancy, until now, at the height of their prosperity, they have also reached appalling depths of moral degradation. . . ." If this corruption was inevitable, it was not unalterable; for its roots were psychic, in the minds and hearts of the people—and, as Sullivan's metaphor suggests, in their failure to think or to build wisely. He called for "fresh air and a general mental sanitation" and pointed out—it was now the burden of all his work—"the life-domain of natural thinking." [5]

The unity of thought and act—the doctrine that thought underlies act and action is thought, that every style, social institution, or form of government is an expression of thought—was the fundamental and difficult lesson Sullivan had to teach. He made it socially relevant in "What is Architecture" by showing how the separation of thought and act, of the theoretical and the practical, had weakened the fabric of society; and whenever he considered the question of styles he taught it, hoping that some day a proper history of architecture would be written with this as its principle. Then the method of classifying styles would be replaced by a method truly historical; forms would be studied in time and place, in relation to the thought they expressed and as an index to civilizations. And then perhaps even the professors would realize what Sullivan meant when he said that all the people constitute the social organism and that architecture is "merely one of the activities of a people and . . . necessarily in harmony with all the others."

Such a history would do for architecture what Holmes had done for the law, and its motto, with slight alterations, might well be his proposition in *The Common Law*—"The life of the law [architecture] has not been logic [styles]: it has been experience." Such a history would also emphasize the fact that life is a process in the course of which all thought and expression change. And it would be welcome because what Sullivan now insisted on was change, its necessity and possibility. The simplest human activity, he claimed, was change—forgetting momentarily his own experience with survivals and what James and Veblen had taught him about habits and habits of thought. But he maintained this, as he explained when proposing this view of history, because "the welfare of democracy is my chief concern in life. . . ." His hopes for democracy and his role as an educator were based on his belief that thought could be changed and that, once altered, it could never again become what it was. "Ever new birth," he said, "never rebirth."

Had Sullivan written this history of architecture his influence might have been greater. But thought for him was act, and he wished to act before feudalism overwhelmed democracy. He had time now for scholarship (he wrote the lengthy paper on natural thinking and the long book on democracy) but neither the inclination nor patience; he preferred to be a critic and a prophet, like Nietzsche, "revaluing . . . our valuations of things. . . ." He would be the "virile critic, human and humane, sensitive to all, and aware of [the] modern daybreak," and he would "weigh the Modern Man in a just balance. . . ." By temperament he was fitted for this role, and it was not that he was a prophet without honor so much as a prophet without an audience that exasperated and for a time silenced him.

When he aproached architecture in this way in "What is Architecture" (the essay which mediates and conveys the spirit of the unpublished "Natural Thinking" and *Democracy*), buildings became "warning hands" and inconsolable voices crying out the perils of the people. Outwardly aristocratic and feudal, they appealed in behalf of democracy—as if their suppressed functions had found utterance; and much of what they said, like the nightmare Sullivan exploited for the purpose of exorcism, might have come from Nordau's *Degeneration*. They bespoke the *fin-de-siècle* feeling of imminent perdition and extinction, that mood of impotent despair which Nordau believed to be the response of the aristocratic sensibility to a dying world. For Sullivan, they told of neurasthenia and hysteria. "In it," he said of this architecture, "is no joy of living—you know not what the fullness of life signifies—you are unhappy, fevered and perturbed." (The transition from buildings to people effectively rendered his idea, that "as are your buildings, so are you.") And this architecture, he claimed in a catalog of symptoms that went beyond Nordau's, was ashamed to be natural and was contemptuous of nature; it was filled with cant and hypocrisy and lacking in serenity, and revealed a want of love for the country and the people. The colossal energy of these buildings was frenzy, not the "true power of equipoise." In them was no evidence of thought concerning the "vital relations of a people." Failing to express this "equilibrium," they signified waste, the social waste of selfishness, the kind of waste Sullivan recognized in the filth and smoke of cities and in the adulteration of food and drugs. Instead they boasted of success and exalted the dollar, and, as Henry James also noted at this time, derided the power of both genuine femininity and genuine masculinity.

The value of this social commentary, which went deeper than most, is to be found in the unity of Sullivan's architectural and social thought. His criteria for social health were those of artistic health; fullness of life, equilibrium of vital relations, serenity and repose—these criteria of art and society rested on the ultimate values of nature. For those accustomed to blander sociological vocabularies, the rhetoric of Sullivan's criticism may be an impediment; in choice of language (and, one might add, in choice of audience) Sullivan demonstrates the difficulties of the artist who engages directly in social criticism. Nevertheless, his criticism is especially valuable because he was an artist and because of the scope of his vision. Like James' criticism in *The American Scene,* which presents linguistic barriers of another kind but also measures society and culture with the criteria of art, it belongs to what might be called the permanent sociology—that science of man which for Sullivan probed both psychic and physical forces.

Words, which Sullivan distrusted, often hide ignorance. (He preferred to communicate with things, as he did in the country banks he began to build at this time. These banks were often richly decorated yet admirably fitted to the needs of the farmers who used them and who felt in them none of the malaise of "art." Here he rendered in stone his belief in democracy—these, in fact, were the minor commissions that kept alive his faith in the people.) But the liability of his rhetoric was different: it hid his knowledge. It did not help him establish his credentials as a social thinker; it did not display the background of his reading and experience. Fervor, for him, was its own testimony. "Look at your body of laws," he exclaimed, "—complicated, grotesque and inefficient, spiked with 'jokers,' as guns are spiked. Look at your Constitution. Does that now really express the sound life in you, or is there a 'joker' in that, too, that is surely strangling you? Look at your business. What is it become but a war of extermination among cannibals?" [6] The passage is typical, closer to Nietzsche than to Holmes, Beard, and Veblen who, in their more reserved ways, were finding in scholarship efficient means for transvaluing the values Sullivan refers to here. But though rhetoric holds sway, there is beneath it, as even this passage shows, a hard core of fact. His experience in Chicago had taught Sullivan much; more than most artists, the architect is enmeshed in society, concerned—as were the editorials of the architectural journals—with industrial, business, and labor problems. (The architectural journals, even those in the West, were conservative. Though Sullivan shared their horror of labor strife and militant reform, his social thought was progressive.) And though he admittedly read for lustres, he had read much, and especially in twentieth century thought.

Photograph by Richard Nickel

Buildings that bug the earth

The National Farmers' Bank, Owatonna, Minn. (1907–08)

"Where did you get these ideas?" the student asks the teacher in *Kindergarten Chats*. "Where anyone with two eyes might have found them," the teacher, no bibliographer, replies. The answer is evasive—so typical of Sullivan that one wonders if such a reply was responsible for George Elmslie's remark that it was "strange he read so few books." [7] But the teacher indicates where "anyone with two eyes" might find them. The most urgent inquiry, he tells the student, is the study of what man has done with his powers. This study includes art, science, metaphysics, poetry, and ethics—it is the "gravitational center" of all the sciences. He calls it "Sociology."

For Sullivan, sociology was twentieth century thought, and for him, as for his contemporaries, it had an aura which it no longer has for us. Sociology, for him, defined a new mode of thought, the genuinely empirical or scientific (natural thinking); a new area of study, the forms and functions of man in society throughout history; and an immediate end in reform— the salvation of man and society: democracy. Sociology, the teacher says, "is the art, the science of gregarious man, the dream of the solitary dreamer, the visionary, the prophet; the world-old dream of the ever dreaming multitudes. Thus is the unitary science, poem and drama of Sociology, the precursor of Democracy—its explorer, its evangel." This feeling for the redemptive possibilities of sociology explains Sullivan's prophetic posture, the way in which he employed the new science in his writings, and his fear lest society let its dreamers perish. And it helps one understand those deep and continuing currents of emotion— those pieties with which ideas are invested—which carried idealism from the transcendentalism of the early nineteenth century to the pragmatism of our own era. [8]

The all-inclusiveness of Sullivan's sociology is matched by the extensiveness of his reading. The student of the *Chats*, if he were still pondering the teacher's ideas in 1909 and attending auctions of books and art-objects (as Sullivan's students actually did for him in the days of success), might have found the answer to his question in the list of Sullivan's books offered for sale by the Williams, Barker, and Severn Company.[9] At first, he would have been confused by the potpourri, perhaps even confirmed in the suspicion that the teacher was a crank with the indiscriminate taste of a village intellectual. But Sullivan, who evidently bought most of what he read, purchased books before he sifted them: sometimes the title, at other times the content, is the clue to his interests. Books like Otto Weininger's *Sex and Character*, which was grossly misogynous and degraded sexuality, or Casper Lavater Redfield's *Control of Heredity*, which advocated the nostrum of late marriage as the guarantee for offspring of intellectual genius, do not substantiate Sullivan's views but indicate both his personal and "sociological" interests. Books such as Max Müller's *Life and Religion*, Renan's *The Apostles*, and Mme. Blavatsky's *Isis Unveiled* show the extent to which he fought the battle between science and religion which Draper's *History of the Intellectual Development of Europe* had not conclusively won; and these books had other uses for Sullivan —*Isis Unveiled*, for example, served him as a history of religious and philosophic thought. A. W. Greeley's *American Weather* and N. S. Shaler's *Aspects of the Earth* suggest the breadth of Sullivan's interest in environment; books on the history of Illinois and on Chicago and its suburbs show his interest in the local milieu; and a number of books—for example, the reports of the Lewis and Clark Expedition and Mayne Reid's novels—reveal the kind of imaginative preparation he believed that the architect must have to commemorate the American past. Books on the history of the English language, on the use of words, on grammar and the teaching of language, are the clue to what the teacher told the student about the nature of words. The many books on music are testimonials of a life-long passion (among the books he left at Ocean Springs is the Chicago Symphony Orchestra program for 1900-1901); and the many books of poetry, among them Chaucer, Shakespeare, Goethe, Whitman, Heine, and Swinburne, and especially Lanier's *The Science of English Verse,* show the lasting effects of Edelman's tutelage and Sullivan's attempt to master another form of expression. The plays of Ibsen would have shocked the student, and the number of German books, particularly the volumes of Goethe, would have puzzled him—for not even the teacher had told him about *Versuch die Metamorphose der Pflanzen zu erklären* and the fragment *Die Natur.* And had he forgotten the Ho-O-Den at the World's Fair and the many articles on Japanese architecture in the journals, the books about Japan and her art might have recalled them and reminded him, as the teacher always had, to look beyond styles to organic affinities.

Many of these books mark old and continuing interests, but most of the books on the auction list belong, even by date of publication, to the kind of sociology Sullivan had in mind when he spoke of twentieth century thought. If the student had overlooked the large collection of art books, he probably would have concluded that the library up for sale belonged to a social thinker rather than to an architect, for the most numerous books dealt either directly or indirectly with the problems of society. Several books were histories—Rawlinson's *Ancient Monarchies,* Breasted's *A History of Egypt,* Buckle's *Civilization in England,* Fiske's *The Critical Period of American History,* McMaster's social and economic *A History of the People of the United States,* and of a more popular kind, Elisha Mulford's *The Nation* and C. C. Coffin's *Redeeming the Republic.* The literature of muckraking was sufficiently represented—John Spargo's *The Bitter Cry of the Children,* Thomas Lawson's *Frenzied Finance,* and Charles Russell's *The Greatest Trust on Earth* are examples. But most of the others dealt with sociology proper: studies of modern science, evolution, and metaphysics like Huxley's *American Addresses,* Haeckel's *The Riddle of the Universe,* Carus' *Fundamental Problems;* treatises on education and psychology like

Alexander Bain's *Education as a Science,* Wundt's *Human and Animal Physiology,* A. F. Chamberlain's *The Child,* G. S. Hall's *Adolescence* and William James' *Psychology;* works on economics and political science like Veblen's *The Theory of the Leisure Class* and *The Theory of Business Enterprise,* Rousseau's *Social Contract,* and Bryce's *The American Commonwealth;* and essays, often sweeping, always prophetic, and most congenial to Sullivan, like Oscar Triggs' *The Changing Order* and H. D. Lloyd's *Man, The Social Creator,* and—waiving its poetic form —Nietzsche's *Thus Spake Zarathustra.*

The departure point of many of these books was the theory of evolution and the conflict between science and theology. One finds in them the new dynamic vocabulary of process, change, adaptation, and transformation, and the notion that the retarding forces in social evolution have been old beliefs, perverted Christianity, and what Haeckel called "the exploded views of the Middle Ages." Science and intellect were the forwarding forces. But, in many, beneath the scepticism was the desire to reconcile science and religion and to ameliorate a brutal naturalism by discovering within it a Christian ethic. Some hoped to reduce the strife of evolutionary society, for which Spencer had been made the apologist, by appealing to altruism—which was either the salvageable part of religion or the result of the evolutionary process itself. Many, having accepted the natural world and its mysteries, were "scientific eulogies of nature," attempts to still old longings with cosmic emotion.[10] Here, as in Haeckel's *The Riddle of the Universe* and Paul Carus' *Fundamental Problems,* there was not only a rejection of utilitarianism and its hedonistic ethics but a scientific affirmation of the oneness of nature; Goethe and Spinoza reappear, and with them, pantheism and a monism of living nature, a monism subsuming both matter and spirit. *Fundamental Problems* best represents Sullivan's metaphysics (Carus had written that "every dualism is

. . . an inconsistency of thought . . .") ; but every book had something for him, even though much of what he read, like Haeckel's *The Riddle of the Universe,* must have been repugnant to him because of its aristocratic bias and avowal of the doctrine of the survival of the fittest.

What he welcomed in the general books on the riddles of the universe was reflected in his own thought and supported his own essentially transcendental—he called it "naturalistic"—metaphysics. They did not supply new ideas so much as sustenance for his mind. They kept him abreast of the stream of evolutionary thought and vindicated his belief in the power of thought, for the present collapse of tradition and authority—as Benjamin Kidd wrote in *Principles of Western Civilization*—was the result of evolutionary theory. Compressing into one generation four centuries of slow change, this theory of change was itself the great instrument of change—and a harbinger of crisis. And for Sullivan it provided a promissory principle. By emphasizing the changing, the future, and the community of man rather than the fixed, the past, or the individual, it opened democratic vistas.

Sullivan recalled in the *Autobiography* that "in Darwin he found much food. The Theory of Evolution seemed stupendous." He noted too that at the time works like Spencer's left him in a haze, but that "what he could grasp he hung on to." Much that he read thereafter, especially books of a metaphysical kind, probably did not dissolve the haze. But Sullivan had grasped enough for his purposes, and, as the *Autobiography* makes clear, his purposes were defined by Draper's belief in science as the liberator of man's spirit and by Edelmann's theory of suppressed functions. Draper fixed the historical cast of his mind. *Democracy: A Man-Search* might be said to be Draper out of the mouth of Nietzsche. But the transit to Nietzsche was by way of the notion of suppressed functions. Not only Nietzsche the prophet, anathematizing the despisers of life, but Nietzsche the psychologist, upholding healthiness and seeking to dispel the fear of life, were imprinted on *Democracy*. And though the *Autobiography* tells nothing about Sullivan's interest in Nietzsche or his even greater interest in psychology, the auction list and his other writings do. The transcendentalist, who exalted creative impulse, had always been a psychologist; the powers and spirit of man were his deepest study; and in the new psychology, perhaps the most important of the evolutionary sciences, he found much to hang on to.

Frank Lloyd Wright always acknowledged his debt to the Centennial Exposition, for there his mother procured the Froebel blocks that turned the kindergarten into a studio for architects. But Sullivan, though his debt was of a different sort, never acknowledged that he owed his introduction to the new psychology to the World's Fair—and to that genuine fair of the intellect, Gothic in architecture but modern in spirit, the University of Chicago. The American Psychological Association was founded in 1892, and two of its members, Joseph Jastrow and Hugo Münsterberg, brought psychology to the Fair by exhibiting its apparatus and setting up a testing laboratory.[11] Nearby, at the University of Chicago, John Dewey established the Chicago School of "functional" psychology, which included the philosophers George Herbert Mead and A. W. Moore, and influenced others in more remote fields, such as Veblen in economics and Jacques Loeb in physiology.

The fundamental tenet of this school, as Dewey explained as early as 1884, was that "the idea of environment is a necessity to the idea of organism, and with the conception of environment comes the impossibility of considering psychical life as an individual, isolated thing developing in a vacuum." As Veblen wrote, "The point of departure of modern psychological inquiry is the empirical generalization that the Idea is Essentially Active." Thinking is the response of an organism to—and within—its environment; it is a constructive activity or function by means of which problems are solved and the environment is altered. It is not an affair of mind and object but of intelligence-environment: all dualisms and elementalism are abandoned. What this meant for Sullivan is perhaps better suggested by Dewey's early statements—that "the true self-related must be the organic unity of the self and the world, of the ideal and the real, and this is what we know of as God," and that "truth, . . . reality, not necessarily *beliefs about* reality, is given in the living experience of the soul's development." [12]

Sullivan's interest in psychology was as catholic as William James'. He went back to Lavater's *Essays on Physiognomy,* and he read books of the order of A. E. Willis' *A Treatise on Human Nature and Physiognomy*—Willis was a self-styled professor, a phrenologist whose book borders on self-help—and T. J. Hudson's *The Law of Psychic Phenomena: A Working Hypothesis for the Systematic Study of Hypnotism, Spiritism, Mental Therapeutics, Etc.* But of greater importance were the books to which the new psychology introduced him, especially those by A. F. Chamberlain, G. Stanley Hall, and William James.

Chamberlain's *The Child: A Study in the Evolution of Man*[13] was a compendious treatise whose central thesis was that "youth was furnished in the order of natural development to the animal as a means of utilizing and controlling the wealth of innate instincts and impulses in a new and higher fashion . . . man especially possess[es] youth because it was necessary to create art (and civilization) from instincts through the transforming power of play." Chamberlain's notion of play as the occupation of the child, as delight in free activity, as constructive and liberating, and as a form of experiment or experience, supported the permissiveness and pedagogy Dewey advocated in *The School and Society* (1899); and his belief that genius is not a neurosis but the normal condition of the child (he cited Goethe's "If children grew up according to early indications, we should have nothing but geniuses") provided a fundamental and democratic principle of education. The evils he wished to remove were adult interference and the thwarting influences of school and environment—the school which was not, as Dewey's was, a proper environment. A garden truly was one in which preindustrial values were recaptured, where the impulse of the child was not misdirected by the predatory motives of competition but permitted to flourish in beneficent communal ways. By relating the flower of civilization to its forgotten seed in the child, Chamberlain's genetic approach effectively transvalued values. It drove both civilization and its discontents back to their origins in the impulse of the child, and it gave education, so often the servant of society, a central role in reform.

The approach of G. Stanley Hall (Chamberlain's colleague) was equally genetic—and idealistic. One might say that Clark University, where Chamberlain was a professor and Hall the president—and from which that captain of education, William Rainey Harper, stole a number of eminent professors for the University of Chicago—was a later-day Concord School of Philosophy. For Hall united Emerson's faith in beneficent nature with Alcott's devotion to education. The clue to his work is contained in his remark that "science justifies the ways of love to man." He was an evolutionary spiritualist and optimist who, by extending evolutionary theory to psychology, hoped to discover "genetic ideas of the soul" and to show that idealism, metaphysics, and religion spring from the basic needs of the soul—indeed, that the soul itself is an evolutionary achievement still in the making. Like Chamberlain he believed that the child is the hope and the light of the world and that all culture and every institution should provide for his nurture.

In turning to adolescence, however, he not only furthered the genetic history Chamberlain began with the child but extended the claims for impulse. His *Adolescence*[14] was one of the great encyclopedias of the age; but for all its science it was a moral tract. He used it to castigate his time for its loss of feeling.

"The heart is parched and bankrupt," he said; "culture represses, and intellect saps the root." The transcendentalists had said as much, and in his language and by citation he acknowledged them. But he also acknowledged Whitman, and without reticence. Adolescence was his area of study because it was the crucial, the great transformation period in human history. It was, he said, "the infancy of man's higher nature, when he receives from the great all-mother his last capital of energy and evolutionary momentum." What made it so important was "the development of the sex function" and the fact that "the sex function is normally . . . the greatest of all stimuli to mental growth." Sexual development, he believed, opened the portal to the ideal world; and like Whitman (and also looking ahead to D. H. Lawrence), he claimed for man and woman alike the paradise that the new psychology promised in the restoration of human nature. "The knowledge of life," he maintained, "is at root the knowledge of love."

His science was also used to justify the transcendentalists' feeling for nature and the general romantic belief that the love of nature is the source of art, literature, science, and religion. Undiminished in force and fervor, the Emersonian-Whitmanian gospel finds new utterance in the chapter on adolescent feelings toward nature. Hall not only cites Emerson and Whitman, he absorbs them: "The spirit of botany is where flowers grow, geology in the fields . . . astronomy . . . in the silence of the open night alone." Nature, he says, is sentiment before it becomes idea, formula, or utility; the adolescent does not need the scientific training of the schools, but rather, as the "genetic pedagogy" proposes (especially in view of the increase in urbanism), an education in the country. Hall reverently explained the child's animistic feelings for flowers and trees. And he insisted that "every youth should be exposed to these sylvan influences in spring, fall, summertide, and winter, for thus all that is best in his nature will ripen and gain ascendancy." Without an occasional day alone in a "city of trees," adolescence, he felt, could never do all of its work.

The ideas of Chamberlain and Hall (and Dewey, who was Hall's student at Johns Hopkins) leave their impress on many of Sullivan's pages and are personified by Grandfather List in the *Autobiography*. Sullivan's father and Moses Woolson, proponents of discipline, take their cues from William James. James, of course, shared—indeed, had been the major source of—the fundamental principles of the new psychology. Much that he wrote in *The Principles of Psychology*[15]—for example, that function makes the organ, or that the pressure creates the channel—appealed to Sullivan. But what apparently appealed to him most was the discussion of habit, attention, and choice. James not only spoke of the economy of habits, he showed how difficult it was to acquire new ones and how important in the battle of life were the discipline and choice that this acquisition required. Habit, he said, "dooms us all to fight out the battle of life upon the lines of our nurture or our early choice. . . ." Like Emerson, he might have said that character is fate; for he, too, had the New Englander's profound sense of character. He showed that choice is an indubitable expression of mind and that "attention and effort are . . . two names for the same psychic fact." He distinguished between knowledge of acquaintance and knowledge about, the latter being the knowledge of the inner nature of the thing, which only attention could secure. He explained genius in terms of sustained attention ("In such minds, subjects bud and sprout and grow."). And for Sullivan, who had been following the growth of the child in Chamberlain and Hall, he added another stage, the years between twenty and thirty which were the most important period for fixing professional and intellectual habits.

What the psychologists did for the study of man, Veblen did for the study of institutions. The genetic approach, applied to institutions, became historicism. The present conflict in society, which Veblen described in terms of business enterprise and industry, was illuminated by history and traced back to its primitive origins in the instinct of workmanship. Man, Veblen said in *The Theory of the Leisure Class*,[16] is an agent, "a center of unfolding impulsive activity"; he is "possessed of a taste for effective work, and a distaste for futile effort." This instinct begets industry—the "effort that goes to create a new thing, with a new purpose given it by the fashioning hand of its maker out of passive ('brute') material. . . ." Veblen found this instinct in its purest form in primitive, archaic societies, those small peaceable, essentially agrarian communities that undoubtedly reminded him of his own early life. These so-called savage societies gave way to a higher form of society, to barbarism, which was characterized by the predatory habit of life. The hunter and the warrior appeared, and "exploit" ("the conversion to his own ends of energies previously directed to some other end by another agent") challenged industry. Prowess, force, and fraud overcame diligence; emulation created an invidious distinction between them; and the leisure class, which with earlier predators "reap[s] where [it has] not strewn," began its long career of dominance, secure in those institutions which enshrined and perpetuated its "habits of thought."

The springs of Veblen's history were psychological. Its protagonist was the instinct of workmanship, a rather unwilling but instinctually indomitable hero at war with futility and waste. This instinct, nothing less than the constructive force in human life, was helped in later accounts by "idle curiosity" and the "parental bent," the one subsuming many of the virtues of play and the other, in its capacity as nurturer of life, the values of altruism. Veblen's irony did not disguise this melodrama, it created it and made his work a morality in which the simple and virtuous hero moved through history put upon by warrior, priest, and captain of industry. One is reminded of Twain's

Yankee mechanic in King Arthur's Court—in fact, Veblen begins by saying that "the institution of the leisure class is found in its best development at the higher stages of the barbarian culture; as, for instance, in feudal Europe. . . ." Everything he says about the leisure class, about its canons of taste, dress, belief in luck, devout observances, and system of higher education, strengthens this connection and points up the lesson of survivals. The hero, with whom Sullivan might have easily identified, finds his instinct of workmanship (Sullivan calls it his will to beneficent power), thwarted on all sides by the reigning feudalism. Instead of the functional canon of beauty, he finds the pecuniary, which Veblen associated with the "reputable usage" of the English upper class; he finds that taste is not satisfied by "structures which in a straightforward manner suggest both the office which they are to perform and the method of serving their end." The leisure class does not want the "aesthetically true" but the "reputably correct"; "novelty," "misspent ingenuity and labor," "conspicuous ineptitude"—all that Sullivan meant by "tasty" buildings—follow. Peaceable traits, such as good nature, equity, and sympathy, he also finds, do not make for success; honesty is not the best policy. And one is even unfitted for struggle, if by chance he is a "brachycephalic-brunet" (as were Veblen and Sullivan) instead of a "dolicho-blond."

Veblen dissected benevolent feudalism only to uncover the lesions of conspicuous waste. His irony helped him remain aloof from actual reforms, but his moral was clear: the end of industry, he said, was "the fullness of life of the individual, taken in absolute terms." This moral was not lost on Veblen's friend, Oscar Lovell Triggs, or on Henry D. Lloyd, the Chicago reformer. His work provided the dark ground of their hope. "We have but to substitute new names for the old ones—competition for anarchy; poverty for the extermination of the conquered . . . ; strikes for internecine war; capitalist for priest and tyrant;

workingmen and farmers for slaves . . . business for conquest.
. . ."—much of what Lloyd said here Veblen had indicated in
The Theory of Business Enterprise. Both Triggs and Lloyd recognized that the battle line of democracy was now the factory and
that the real problems of American life were industrial. By
ennobling labor and preaching love they tried to lessen industrial
strife. They supported the social movement, that tendency in
modern life which, Lloyd maintained, "is making brothers out
of competitors, republicanising private wealth and power . . .
democratising common labour for common welfare . . . pro-
claiming that in the labour world, as everywhere, love is the
law." Democracy was their religion; they worked for conversion, for life, as Triggs said, "on wholly new terms." [17]

It is easy to mock these men of good hope, as Veblen sometimes
did, until one remembers that such men filled the reservoir of
democratic aspiration from which all subsequent generations
have drawn. Their hopes were not altogether sentimental; their
sense of crisis was genuine. Lloyd believed that in his day there
was more discontent than at the time of the French Revolution;
he felt that American society was approaching one of the great
crises of history, or, as he put it when looking forward hopefully, "we are in the rapids of a new era." Triggs called his book,
The Changing Order: A Study of Democracy, and the title of
Lloyd's, *Man, The Social Creator,* brought together many strands
of the new thought that had made democracy a social goal and
man himself the agent of this destiny.

When Sullivan spoke of sociology as the explorer and evangel
of democracy, he was thinking of books of this kind and possibly
of his friend Oscar Lovell Triggs. A disciple of William Morris,
Triggs was an active member of the Illinois Industrial Arts
League—where, most likely, he first met Sullivan. But Triggs
was also a devoted student of Whitman (his fame today rests
on his contribution to the *Complete Writings of Walt Whitman*
published in 1902) and an eager advocate of the art of democ-

racy. His aesthetics, uniting the traditions of Morris and Whitman, was social: art is "social in its origin, social in its nature, and social in its results." He believed that Frederick Law Olmsted was America's greatest artist and that "after Olmsted, our most distinctive artist is Sullivan, an architect." He celebrated the functional architecture of the Chicago School, extolled the superior value of Sullivan's work ("more than any other builder . . . [he] founds his work in personal character and personal responsibility and permeates them with poetic feeling"), cited Sullivan's writing to support his own views of democratic art, and confirmed Sullivan's indictment of the World's Fair. No one praised Sullivan more highly or more nearly in the way Sullivan wished, for Triggs placed him not only as an artist but as a social reformer, as an example of the modern artist who believed that art was both individual expression and social wealth. Sullivan's work and thought supported Trigg's belief that, since art and life are intimately connected, "it is doubtful if anyone can either create or understand great [art], who has not the genius for social reform."

In *The Changing Order,* Sullivan found himself in the company of the worthies of the age. This high estimate of his work was but part of his debt to Triggs; he owed him more for help in finding his way to the new thought and perhaps still more for the incentive to undertake in his writing the work of reform. Triggs was a docent in literature at the University of Chicago. His sociological mentor was Veblen (along with Lester Ward). He knew Dewey. He had the key to the University and, as his book shows, he had opened many of its doors. Sullivan did not follow him everywhere—he was too antipathetic to feudalism, for example, to accept Triggs' view that in the Middle Ages labor was art. But much of *The Changing Order* fortified his thought and focused it. Secure in his evolutionary faith, Triggs swept through history in order to announce the advent of democracy, the next step in evolution and historic development.

He canvassed the new psychology, education, and art, and related philosophic monism and the new aesthetics to the social movement. He opposed democracy to feudalism, the creative aspects of labor and play to leisure, and the "esoteric" to the "exoteric." Feudalism and aristocracy, for him, represented external authority, an imposed order; democracy represented the ascendancy of an internal order, the "complete utterance and exercise" of the people in every form of human activity. In discussing this change from outer to inner order, Triggs employed the older transcendental vocabulary of "correspondence" as well as the newer vocabulary of functionalism. He cited not only his great men of the day, Dewey and Sullivan, but Emerson, Whitman, Inness, and Lincoln in America, and Burns, Wagner, Tolstoi, Ruskin, Morris, and Millet in Europe. In his hands, the history of art became a history of the fully developing personality. All the artists he considered were apostles of reform; all contributed to the doctrine of man which Whitman had made the spiritual basis of democracy—"I am only he who places over you no master, better, God, beyond what waits intrinsically in yourself." Triggs' book made Sullivan aware of his place in this tradition and kept before him the grandeur of his mission.

And so did *Man, The Social Creator*. Henry D. Lloyd, as Jane Addams and Anne Withington noted, had spent his life in searching out the "newer phases of the democratic spirit," and now, in this book which they prepared for publication, was tracing "the source and growth of religious motives in contemporaneous society." He had always been a religious thinker. That man was the creator and redeemer of himself and society, that the motive power of redemption was love and reciprocity the law— these were his fundamental beliefs, and reason enough for his editors' associating him with Emerson. Love, he claimed, was a natural force, the combining force; hate was the separating force. In the world of life, love worked as gravitation and electricity did in the world of matter. It needed only good conductors, sympathetic people, and free institutions; or—in an equally popular metaphor—"It is as safe to love as to plant seeds in the garden." Love was latent in humanity, the common people were its reservoir. Broadening with the stream of evolution, love found its outlet in work or "service." Where love was the force, work was the manifestation—and the universal religion. "The Kingdom of heaven," Lloyd said, "is not to be taken by storm but by day's labour." He called mankind to the Church of the Deed.

The religious rhetoric of Lloyd's book charged such seemingly neutral words as "the instinct of workmanship." Selfishness and unselfishness, stripped of the moral overtones that often make them unacceptable (how hard it is to talk of love, when, as Lloyd said, the words themselves had to be redeemed for use), are as good as force and fraud and diligence. Lloyd knew as well as Veblen the realities of "selfish education, selfish politics, selfish industry . . . the three persons of Baal of our modern world." Irony has no special efficacy as rhetoric, and the health it restores by purgation at times needs to be strengthened by open convictions conveyed in accents of faith. From Veblen Sullivan learned to see society clearly but men like Lloyd quickened his faith in the religion of democracy. When he wrote *Kindergarten Chats* he anticipated his role as a Messiah. The great, immediate task, he said, was the "search for Man": "current ideas concerning democracy are so vague, and current notions concerning man's powers so shapeless, that the man who shall clarify and define, who shall interpret, create, and proclaim in the image of Democracy's fair self, will be the destined man of the hour: the man of all time." He had already envisaged the great work for which his reading prepared him, and now, with nothing to create but much to interpret and proclaim, he undertook it, fired anew perhaps by the words of Mazzini which Lloyd cited—"The first one who makes a religion of Democracy will save the world."

Sullivan's concept of natural thinking was the central idea of *Democracy: A Man-Search*. Whenever he speaks of meeting reality "face to face," one of the themes and refrains of *Democracy,* he wishes to call attention to natural thinking. It is his greatest, the primary inversion that makes possible the change from feudalism to democracy; it marks the modern era and is an event in human history comparable to the Copernican discovery. "Rapidly," he said in "Education," "we are changing from an empirical to a scientific attitude of mind; from an inchoate to an organic trend of thinking."[18] How well he understood twentieth century thought—that rejection of the limited empiricism of the British tradition (which Morton White calls the revolt against formalism)[19] for a philosophy of experience. He impugned logic, preferring an account of how men actually think; he replaced formalism with historicism; and he considered culture organically, as a living totality. His own building and writing exemplified this scientific attitude and organic trend of thinking. It brought forward the earlier philosophy of experience he had found in Whitman and merged it with the later philosophy of men like James and Dewey, and, as nowhere else in his day, it fused inextricably the idea of the organic with the idea of democracy. For democracy, Sullivan believed, was more than political. It had nothing to do with the abstract notion of man's natural rights but everything to do with his actual natural powers; it was a way of thought and life, a way of using one's powers creatively, honestly, naturally—and socially. And Sullivan placed all of his hopes on it because his thesis, as he said in *Democracy,* was "that man creates in the image of his thought. . . ."

This thesis was tentatively explored in "Natural Thinking: A Study in Democracy," [20] a manuscript of 162 pages from which Sullivan prepared the paper he delivered before the Chicago Architectural Club on February 13, 1905. According to *The Inland Architect,* this paper was Sullivan's best, and, when restored to its original length, a study which would contribute significantly to American thought.[21] Much that he discussed in "Natural Thinking" was taken up in *Democracy,* a better organized and often imaginatively realized work which he probably felt compelled to write because the discursive exposition of "Natural Thinking" did not sufficiently help men to *see.* It was not enough to tell them, he would show them, would dramatize the choice between inverted (feudal) and natural (democratic) thinking on which the destiny of mankind depended. The dramatization was often effective, weakened primarily by length and nagging insistence, and its major deficiency for those interested in Sullivan's thought was its omission of the close analysis of natural thinking and the discussion of "publicity" which the earlier manuscript provided.

From the time of his essay on "Inspiration," Sullivan had been trying to impart the lesson of natural thinking. He had not been especially successful; he had not rendered the experience as fully as Whitman had. But what Whitman had taught him (and modern psychologists had confirmed) and what he had learned from his own experience formed the bases of his analysis. Natural thinking presupposes the continuity of man and nature (or the environment)—the child who goes forth everyday. The universe and man are one (William James said that man's faculties, emotions, and instincts are adapted to the world). Under normal conditions, that is, before "feudal" philosophers divide the powers of man into faculties, man is a unified sensibility, one with—a phase of—life (as Emerson wrote: "the currents of the Universal Being circulate through me. . . ."). Most of man's "thought" is subconscious or instinctual; the forces of life think for him if he lets them (Emerson: "I expand and live in the warm day like corn and melons.").[22] Sullivan's analogy is the complex process of walking (he was familiar with Eadweard Muybridge's photographic studies of motion). Mind is not a separate thing nor is thinking a special process; thinking cannot be arrogated by an elite. Thinking is a common power and activity and it has its origins in the desire and consent of the mind. When man consents, when he willingly opens the channels of his senses, when he chooses to be receptive, to be a "conductor" (a common metaphor of the day), then natural thinking prevails. The senses are the portals to the inner man, to the body, brain, heart, and soul—the agencies of response. Man's power as a creator depends not only on receptivity or sensation but on the depth of his response, on the degree of consent or attention. He must not only hear but listen (as Woolson had instructed his pupils); he must actively attend, permit himself "a certain responsive ripening." (Emerson distinguished between "superficial seeing" and the "attentive eye.") [23] When the brain consents, one sees objectively; when the heart consents, one has the "finer vision" of sympathy; when one fully consents with the soul, one has spiritual insight. Opening completely to life, one becomes a part of it, until one loses "that separateness and identity which is at once the source and sustenance of consciousness"; as Emerson said, "all mean egotism vanishes";[24] and one learns, as Whitman had, that the "kelson of creation is love." [25] One is empowered by life to do the beneficent work of life.

Democracy is consonant with this psychological liberation. It requires that man come into the "open," that he free his powers. It would establish man's equipoise, the balance between what man finds within him and without him; it would make him at home in the universe, secure his "anchorage." And it would do this by removing fear—the fundamental cause of his inverted thinking, of the malady of the ideal, and, as Nietzsche said, of the *ressentiment* that transforms the naturally beneficent (the "bestowing virtue") into maleficent power. It would loosen "the mind-forg'd manacles" Blake heard in London and Sullivan in "The Great City" (Chicago). By means of "publicity" it would open the dark recesses of secrecy, held fast by those who tyrannize over the minds of men.

Since democracy is a psychological condition, its achievement requires a therapy deeper than political reform. Conversion is needed, a new faith in man, a yea-saying to life. To this end, Sullivan advocated publicity; for publicity was communication, and communication would make for mental sanitation. Education, as he considered it, was the primary instrument of publicity: it would not only lead the child in the way of natural thinking, but would confront the adult throughout his life with the new thought; and even more important for the openness of democracy, it would provide an outlet for man's desire to communicate or share the impulses of his heart.

History, too, as the proponents of the "new history" believed, was publicity. It became a means of enlightenment when the past was used to explain the present, and it became a weapon of democracy by pointing out those crises which for Sullivan were the "parting of the ways." This was the way in which Sullivan used history in *Democracy* and in "Natural Thinking." In the latter, moreover, he used history—especially that of the centuries following the Renaissance—to trace the advances in publicity itself: the new science, the new political forms like democracy, and the new instruments of communication. He wished to show, as Whitman had in "Passage to India," that communication had made the world smaller and had bound the world together. The means for communicating democratic thought and aspiration were at hand; means that he believed would make—were making—the choice between feudalism and democracy the immediate issue not only in America but throughout the world. (He prophesied the Russian Revolution and the awakening of the Orient.) In studying history he had embraced the world; he was no longer a nationalist; and though he continued to battle for an American architecture, he did not do so for chauvinistic reasons. Because of communication, he felt that "Democracy cannot be throttled"; and because art, too, was publicity, he felt that the victory of living forms in America would be a victory for the world.

Sullivan did not overestimate the power of communication; he merely forgot one lesson of history in emphasizing another. He forgot the Inquisition, that attempt to throttle the new science of the Renaissance. His faith in publicity had been strengthened by the aggressive attacks of the muckrakers and by those "upright men" (the men of good hope) who were renewing the claims of justice and honesty. Like himself, they were in the "middle," caught between the monopolies of business and the monopolies of labor, but still free and willing to speak out. He did not foresee a monopoly of communication nor the manipulative uses of publicity. He thought that the men in the middle (not necessarily of the middle class), those men who accepted the office of the American Scholar, would always leaven society. He believed with Altgeld that "Wherever there is a wrong, point it out to all the world, and you can trust the people to right it." [26] That was why, as publicist, as artist and educator, he did not assert too much when he said that "toward the making of a new era, I have done somewhat of my share."

Henry Adams, at the World's Fair, had pondered on the steps beneath Richard Hunt's dome "almost as deeply as on the steps of Ara Coeli, and much to the same purpose." Like Adams, Sullivan saw the imperial façade and pondered its meaning. He, too, realized that "Chicago asked in 1893 for the first time the question whether the American people knew where they were driving." And he, too, realized, but was unwilling to accept as Adams had, the fact that a "capitalistic system had been adopted. . . ." [27] He did not think that everything Veblen had disclosed in *The Theory of Business Enterprise* was unalterable, and he proposed, by writing the history of democracy, once more to put the question of 1893 to the people. He would make a Clopet demonstration, reduce all to simples, to feudalism and democracy, and determine the people's choice. "The main and the immediate business of democratic philosophy," he wrote in *Kindergarten Chats*, "is to simplify, to clarify and to know itself." He would do what studies such as *Communitas* and *The City in History* have done: show alternatives and the consequences of choice. He would not wait with Adams nor ask "how long?" He would not be a meliorist like Triggs and Lloyd. As his examiner in history at the Beaux Arts had prophesied, he would "turn the teachings of history upside down";[28] and, if a book, if publicity could do it, he would free the people from fear and fate.

The book, *Democracy: A Man-Search*, was never published in Sullivan's lifetime.[29] Only now can its force, the tremendous vitality and imagination with which he endowed it, be measured. Though not likely to be taken, as Professor Morrison suggested it might be, for "one of the great literary achievements of modern times,"[30] it is still a singular work. Its structure is firm; its ideas are often imaginatively rendered; and occasionally the prose is as skillful, sure, and vibrant as Melville's. Its theme—man's search for man in history—is perhaps the greatest, its method—the psychological—perhaps the profoundest, its intent—the desire to redeem man—perhaps the most passionate, and compassionate. Though it is marred by repetition, especially toward the end, and the effect seems to be shrillness, it is boldly conceived and written with restraint. It anticipates much in modern literature in its use of archetypes, in its fusion of past and present, in its richness and complexity. There is nothing conventional about it except the lapses into rhetoric; it is an original artistic solution to the problem of communicating the new sociology, indelibly marked by Sullivan's individuality and genius.

The imaginative center of the book is "Dance of Death"

(Group II, Chapter 5). It begins with "A Child's Tale," the first of several fables, whose serious import Sullivan explained in "Revolution" (Group I, Chapter 5). Stories—he cites the Bible and the "gossamer weavings of the finely creative oriental mind," suggesting something of his own ornament—he says, are perennial symbols; they always mean "now" and in the living solvent of their spirit all men become alike. The child's tale tells of identity; it is the story of children who go forth, who become flowers and butterflies, and whose parents become the eagles of Whitman's "The Dalliance of the Eagles." It is a story of simple life in nature, of life close to the earth in the gladness of the morning. But it is a story of long ago, told in a strange tongue.

It is followed by another fable, "A Tale O' the Moor," a "grown folks' tale," told centuries after in another land. (Sullivan probably heard a similar tale from Julia, the Irish hired girl on the List's farm.) This ghost story is a tale of the horror of night, of superstition and fear; of a wayfarer who falls asleep in a graveyard, awakens at midnight to the dance of death of thirteen ghosts, and dies of terror. The wayfarer is everyman; he will become Sullivan's "man on the street," even Christ; and he is not saved, as Sullivan had previously hoped he would be, by the cock crow of the dawn. He is not saved because, like those who hear the tale and whose terror-stricken appeals to God intensify it, he is the victim of his own fears. He lives in the phantasmal world of feudalism.

In the next episode, "Interlude," the setting is contemporary civilization, when men, supposedly, are no longer afraid of the night or motivated by fear. Like "The Man on the Street" and "The Great City"—the chapters which enclose "Dance of Death" in a frame of realism—it tells of a civilization that kills and crucifies for money, and thus enacts its own dance of death. "Interlude" is a dialogue in which the narrator's "outrageous" condemnation of modern civilization is answered by the denials of the "man on the street." His replies, ironically, often give the substance of the narrator's deepest hopes and hold up in support of them the very institutions he condemns. The irony is bold and telling, a proper weapon for cant and hypocrisy; and when the man on the street mouths sanctimonious platitudes, the dialogue fades into a poem, called "The Dance of Death," which reveals his interior thoughts, the reality his words and "pious leer" have tried to hide:

> We circle—around—the man at bay!—
> The luckless wight that falls our way!—
> The man who thinks that we're not here!
>
> . . . .
>
> A man—they nailed—
> Upon a cross—
> It is our gain—
> It was his loss;
>
> . . . .
>
> High Christ—upon—the cross—was fixed—
> He with—the money—changers—mixed!

The poem concludes with the admonition to speak quietly, to keep silent, for

> Some man you meet—
> Out in the street—
> (Might get to thinking—rather hard and—disagreeably)
> And it would be
> (Scarce wise to set his eyes on things he has no business whatsoe'er
> to know)

The narrator is advised that if he must tell stories, he should "make them nice."

The tale that follows, in spite of its utopian form, is not nice. It is "A Traveler's Tale"—"a man's tale! A story . . . told in tranquility; in a spot not on the map, maybe—but surely open to the earth and air and sky." One can imagine Mr. Homos, the Altrurian in Howells' utopian romances, telling it. Indeed, Sullivan used Howells' earnest but amiable work to his own ends throughout the book. Phrases, like "too busy," "money talks," and "business is business," become dark refrains in *Democracy;* they are vulgar phrases, often unexamined by those who use them; but, like the colloquial voice of literary realism, they shatter the complacency of polite, conventional speech. The very existence of two voices is one of the paradoxes the traveler notes.

The traveler in Sullivan's tale has returned from America to a land where children have flowers, birds, and trees as their friendly companions; his Altruria is the land of "A Child's Tale." His narrative tells of Sullivan's own amour with America, and, as in Howells', of the glaring paradoxes of the civilization he finds there. He tells his friends of the vast and beautiful country— "Never was a great multitude placed in so free, so expansive, so adequate, so bountiful, gracious and simple a setting." He tells of a land without famine; a land webbed by communication and interchange; a land of schools and universal literacy; a land where social castes are not acknowledged and men are free to vote, speak, and worship; a land whose people are immensely energetic. But instead of "life-results of simple noble, strong and fruitful harmony," the cities are "blemishes" on the fair face of the land, and the throngs in the cities—with their "universal type of face" ("a face with features singularly decomposed, disorganized and sordid")—prompt his search, as they did Sullivan's, for what lies beneath the paradox. He notices the superficial brusqueness and affability of speech that hide the real man, the lack of genuine spirituality, and the manifest anxiety that accounts for the reckless overuse of drugs and drink. Finding the food adulterated, he looks to the mental food, and discovers that it is "tainted" with feudalism. "That was enough!"

he says. "With a feudal philosophy, a feudal doctrine of economics, and a feudal religion as guides, the rest of the way was clear." Now he understands what the institutions veil, now he begins to see the meaning of double lives and the vacant faces of the phantoms he meets in the streets. Democracy has turned to hell: "Truly my heart turned faint as I saw them, day by day, moving their devitalized bodies and their gray, poisoned minds. No sadder, no more tragic spectacle is to be viewed . . . than that of these dreamers of putrid dreams, floating, like unwelcome dregs. . . ."

The feudal taint, he learns from American history, had existed from the beginning—in Negro slavery. It now exists in "white serfdom." The schools and churches ("The preachers were mere social parasites, kept by the well-to-do and the rich, like so many kept women") foster it. In fact, the entire "system" does: it is a confidence game ending in betrayal. Commercialism, with its law of "dog eat dog," is the real object of American life; the common ideal is selfishness. If fate (which the traveler does not believe in) has made a trap for western civilization, this is it; for gold is "the little bait with which their mighty trap is baited." When he thinks of this, he is reminded of a "trivial" tale he has heard—the "Tale O' the Moor." For him, its most interesting detail is the cock crow: "The crowing of that cock at dawn, the ringing, jubilant, awakening voice of chanticleer, must have stood, within the darkened minds of those past and gone people as a symbol of hope, as a . . . mystic herald of a brighter day. . . ." And having linked the dance of death of the tale with that of American life, he wonders if a cock will crow a new dawn in America.

His hopes are few: the land itself, the fact that he has heard voices crying in the wilderness, and the promptness with which Americans, when once they see, put thought into action. He hopes against hope; the logic of American civilization all but shatters his faith in nature and in man. For his conclusions portend a "psychological hour" when, should America fail to respond to the cock crow, civilization itself will come to "its sure swift downfall." Then "savagery, unloosened, will become brute real, instead of artificial; and, in their mad and sanguinary orgy, they will vanish exhausted, from the earth, to join the fading caravan of the past, moving into the abysmal dusk." The traveler has seen the falling towers, the hooded hordes, the unreal cities; he has heard the reminiscent bells and the voices singing out of empty cisterns and exhausted wells. Still he hopes "with all the ardor of the love I bear mankind." He speaks for Sullivan, who, perhaps following Thoreau, was himself chanticleer, "crowing the shrillest dawn that the world has known."

Every part of *Democracy* is representative of the whole. In the "Introduction," as in Whitman's "Inscriptions," the themes are announced. The reader is to enter a theatre, to see the unfolding drama of man's dreams; to see on the stage of time, now brightly lit, now dark, the folly of "man's self-eclipse." Every episode is both past and present. "Man has stood, and stands," Sullivan says, "isolated, a wanderer, a stranger in his own history; far from a God, far from Man, far from Self,—even while seemingly so close, so vividly close to Earth, and Self, and Gods, and Man." The very search to find out "how and why this was so, and still is so" will itself dramatize the power of thought which, for Sullivan, is the protagonist—hero and villain—of history. What man has dreamed, he has built. The how and why are to be found in his dreams, his thoughts. By searching where hitherto he has failed to look— in himself—man will find the spring of history. For history is not an external force. It is not fate or destiny, but the stuff of dreams. The searcher must be, as Sullivan had increasingly become, a psychologist.

As a psychologist of the culture of fear, Sullivan did not err in locating the essential symptom. The book begins with a chapter entitled "What is the Use?" This cry of futility, later identified as the voice of feudalism, is the book's refrain; it summons a negative vision: of nihilism, of death, and of the illusion of hope. It is the cry of the past and the cry of the present. And it is dramatized by the specter who first utters it. Having come to the door he wishes to open, the searcher is stopped by the specter who guards it. He is told that there is no door, only the wall raised by Fate; that others have looked for the door and have been crucified; that if he intends to make a book into a door, to show men that they themselves have reared the wall and to turn them to the man-search, he, too, will be rended. But the searcher, who for the moment is Siegfried, does not heed the warning. He chooses otherwise, for he knows that choice itself will rout the Great Denier. The only answer to the spectral questioner is choice. That is the burden of "The Point of the Ways" (Group I, Chapter 2): one must give his "life-force" either to feudalism or to democracy.

How the wall was reared and the specter came to stand there is told in "Night and Day," a brilliant recreation of the primitive, prehistorical origins of dualistic thought. Once men were children in the garden of the world; they went forth every day; and they marveled at the mysteries of day and night. Feeling their own smallness and fragility in the presence of these forces, they externalized and deified them. In their need for security, they created gods—as later, in their need for explanations, they created philosophic systems. Though they were "pioneers" and therefore worthy of respect, they alienated themselves from the world and divided themselves by projecting everywhere the polarity of thir thought. In the system of Zoroaster, which serves as a later example, man's life (the unity of all within and without) was split "through the center as with a glittering axe, and That which is One, fell asunder." All subsequent "gorgeous fabrics" of thought that men hang as veils between themselves and the unknown are woven from this archetypal pattern.

The "Too Busy" of the next chapter is simply the excuse of a restless people who refuse to investigate real things and whose empty activity masks their own anxieties. They prefer to evade the implications of the previous chapters—that man creates in the image of his thought and is responsible for his choice. But the searcher will not accept their excuse. He will bring them "face to face" by tracing act to thought; and he will place the responsibility for that thought on them by showing that they themselves dictate the thought of the eminent and even in their apathy choose what that thought shall be. (One of Sullivan's most significant inversions, no longer startling in an age of public opinion surveys, is that the powerful, rich, and eminent are begotten by and beholden to the multitudes.) The final chapter of the section, "Revolution," is subtitled "A Turning-Movement" in order to suggest Sullivan's own alternative to violent change. It instructs the reader in the nature of words, fable, and history, and prepares him for what is to follow.

The first group of chapters, "Parting of the Ways," is introductory and preparatory. The second group, "Face to Face," treats the searcher's philosophy and some of the signs of the present time. The third group, "The Man of the Past," begins the historical search which advances, by way of "Dreams" (Group IV), to "The Man of Today" (Group V). The search concludes in the final group, "The New Way," which considers the powers of man. The search is not as devious as it seems; the historical excursions are really applicable to the present, as much a part of the searcher's consciousness as are the historical flights of "Song of Myself." In fact, the general plan and some portions of the book suggest Whitman's work. Sullivan assumes that all men, past and present, are alike. He seeks the kind of self-recognition which for Whitman makes for health and the possibility of the democratic life of sympathy. He wishes to take man into himself that he may know the "Me myself" and utter its affirmation of life. The reader is often addressed as "you" and taken in hand. The searcher hopes to clear his conventional vision, to leave him in the "open." Then, he promises, "I shall, myself, dissolve"; the reader will be left alone, empowered by his experience, ready to choose the new way of the open road. Like *Kindergarten Chats, Democracy* is open-ended, not concluding an experience so much as challenging the reader with new possibilities of experience. Both end with "NOW BEGIN!"

The search is neither as easy nor as simple as one might infer from the melodramatic opposition of feudalism and democracy. These terms are used "for most pressing purposes of reinforcement"; they are not catchwords. The entire book explores their complex meanings. Philosophically, their equivalents are dualism and monism; psychologically, the abstracting intellect and Reason (intellect in union with the heart); psychically, the abnormal ego and the Ego, the sum of all man's liberated powers; medically, disease and health; morally, selfishness and selflessness, betrayal and honesty, malevolence and benevolence; politically, absolutism and democracy; socially, individualism and community. One leads to a feeling of despair, the other to optimism; one affirms death, the other life; one is an endless seeking and wandering, the other a homecoming. Each is judged by its conception of God, for "the God-conception is ever in exact accord with the social conception." One conceives of an absolute hierarchical God whose law is might makes right, the other has no God separate from itself, for it is one with the silent, gentle "Integrity of Life." Feudalism and democracy ramify in meanings with the great complexity of what the searcher sees, but in their usual opposition they measure that complexity by reminding one of the simplicity at the heart of things.

If "Dance of Death" is the imaginative center of the book, "The Nazarene" and "Story of the Church" (Group IV, Chapters 3 and 4) are its sociological center. For both are immediately relevant, and realize concretely the meanings of feudalism and democracy. The story of Christ, who more than anyone is the hero of *Democracy*, serves several purposes. His advent is an example of the fructifying dream of the multitudes and of the emergence of new life out of despair. After the long night of history, during the period of Imperial (feudal) Rome, Christ announced for the first time the gospel of democracy. His gospel was betrayed, partly because it came too soon (the world was not ready for it as it is now), but chiefly because it was woven into the fabric of feudal thought. The Church, the great betrayer at this turn in history, was the supreme artificer of gorgeous fabrics. God-making was its business. Here, in fact, was a "business enterprise," a "paragon monopoly and trust," a political "machine," superior to those of the present. The Church "knew its business." Founded on fraud and upheld by cunning, seemingly secure because of its monopoly of learning and its "organization," it prevailed for centuries, until new thought (Arabic science) destroyed it. Its "magnates" had become recklessly arrogant; with the Inquisition they tried to suppress "publicity," and they failed. They chose wealth and power instead of the free spirit of man, but they could not escape "the all-inclusive law of internal compensation." What they had done brought its own inevitable reaction.[31]

Feudalism is the old dream of man, democracy the new. The old dream accounts for the history of man from the beginning; with changes only in superficial values, its formula suits "the epoch, the century or the generation." [32] The man of today—"The Practical Man," "The Eminent Man," "The Self-Made Man," "The Politician," "The Parasite," "The Monopolist"—is the man of the past. But there are new dreams to be dreamed when "we are all widest awake." These are the dreams that the bright modern light irradiates and that the new thought fills with a new image of man, with a new day and its new achievements. The new thought has dissolved the phantasms of the past; it has defined man's real nature; it urges the creative powers within him and sets him dreaming of a new civilization. It teaches man what Whitman had taught—that man's best dependence is upon humanity itself and his own "inherent, normal, full-grown qualities";[33] it teaches what Emerson had taught— that "the impoverishing philosophy of ages has laid stress on the distinctions of the individual, and not on the universal attributes of man." [34] It conclusively identifies organic thought with the democratic rather than with the hierarchical. Celebrating life and creativity, it opens the door in the wall of Fate.

Of all the parables in *Democracy*, perhaps the one that expressed Sullivan's deepest hope was "A Child's Tale." Embodying his dream of "human sunshine and gladness . . . the joy of efficiently living and of efficiently doing" and his dream of radiant health, courage, and "gentle, manly, spiritual integrity," it recalls that simple time when men satisfied their instinct of workmanship. Its obvious contrast is the ghost story, the "grown folks' tale." It connects *Kindergarten Chats* and the *Autobiography* and explains why Sullivan ultimately measured civilization in terms of the child. That men were reluctant to initiate the child in the ways of their civilization was the mark of failure; that civilization revered and fostered the wholeness of the child was the mark of its success. The child was life, the seed: his hope. If he could show, as Thoreau had done, that the soil was still fertile and would bear men, then perhaps the renewal of life that was the promise of democracy would have a surer foundation. He lived in that hope and the specter at the door did not silence him. When he wrote the *Autobiography* he did not glorify himself; he wrote of the child who went forth every day and who, coming to manhood, created in the image of his thought.

5: A BACKWARD GLANCE

Remember the seed-germ.
Sullivan, A System of Architectural Ornament
According with a Philosophy of Man's Powers

"As for me," Sullivan wrote to one of his former draftsmen at the end of 1917, "the bottom has dropped out, and the future is a blank." [1] Unable to procure war work, forced to move to even dingier rooms in the Auditorium Building, the aging architect knew in idleness (and from the bitterness of loneliness and failing health) the truth of what he had said in *Democracy* —"It is not now good weather for prophets." When, urged by Bragdon, he revised *Kindergarten Chats* in 1918, he acknowledged the season of his own despair. In "Winter," he had called upon an unanswering God: "Have I not lived for my art? Must then I die for it? And, dying, leave nought behind else a few precious, scattered seeds, overlaid with snow—when my heart was so filled with fertility . . . ?" "Why," he implored, "dost thou bring agony to them that bring forth in thy name?" He knew the winter when there is "no strength; no spirit; no breath"; he feared the barren landscape, the sorrowful spectacle of "a leafless art in which the sap has ceased to flow." And only by adding the poetic exaltation of "Spring Song" (much of which recaptures the creed of "Life and Love" he had proclaimed in the earlier poems of "Nature and the Poet") did he restore the equipoise of his faith and summon the courage to "be virile to the end!"

During these years he was haunted by the idea of degeneration. Evolutionary theory, which supported his intuition of the rhythm of life and death, postulated devolution—disorganization as well as organization. The many psychological studies he had read were unanimous in charting the stages of life from infancy through childhood and adolescence to maturity (generally ending at 60 years) and old age and degeneration. Haeckel, for example, wrote that "Man's psychic life runs the same evolution—upward progress, full maturity, and downward degeneration—as every other vital activity in his organization." [2] But, ill as he was with heart disease, Sullivan would not admit this. He did not wish to be the Ancient of the *Autobiography* who "doddered down the road dustily regurgitating the thoughts of his childhood now become decayed and senile. . . ." Though he spoke rather sadly of "those days" of eminence when paying tribute to Adler in "Development of Construction" (1916),[3] he told another story in the *Autobiography*.

There he wrote another version of the man-search, a fable of youth that portrayed the upward progress of man as he had followed it in the work of Chamberlain, Hall, and James. That was its explicit purpose, for he believed with Charles Whitaker (the editor of the *Journal* of the American Institute of Architects who solicited the *Autobiography* and drew its moral for contemporary civilization) that "the reorganization of child life has [become] the only possibility there is." [4]

But personally he looked forward to spring by glancing backwards to childhood. Both the theme and the activity of writing were restorative. He had learned that to be forever in possession of childhood was the mark of genius; and he glorified Michelangelo not so much because he had created on *momentum* but because he had maintained his powers undiminished into old age. The high value he placed on the *Autobiography* and *A System of Ornament According with a Philosophy of Man's Powers,* the companion volumes of his last years, was due to more than their intrinsic excellence or their importance in forwarding the cause of democracy: they vindicated his faith in himself. One enacted the growth of his unwavering belief in the universal beneficent creativity of man and the other demonstrated in his chosen medium his unfailing skill and the irrepressible fertility of his imagination. Both were proofs of health—of the courage to overcome illness and to rout despair with art. As always, creativity was his mode of conquering.

Both are remarkable books. But the more remarkable is *A System of Ornament.*[5] Not only does it most succinctly state Sullivan's basic ideas, it also visualizes them. It is a treatise on man, on the act of creation as the ripest fulfillment of his powers—all by way of elucidating and exemplifying the principles of his personal grammar of ornament. Here the artist justifies in the beneficent power of art the claims he had made for the powers of man. He shows how the soul blends harmoniously with materials, how "nothing is really inorganic to the creative will of man" who has the power to transmute everything into the image of his passion: the power to create that "which was hitherto nonexistent"—a human environment, his own secure anchorage. Man is a life-giver, and where there is man nothing need be without life. Creation is his highest and his most common form of activity.

The source of this vital power is the ego, the unity of all of man's physical, mental, emotional, moral, and spiritual powers. It is comparable to the germ of the seed which is the "seat of identity" and which contains the "will to live," the pressure which ever seeks its full expression in form. *A System of Orna-*

ment shows the seed seeking its form in efflorescence; the *Auto-biography* shows the similar growth of the child and the efflorescence of an idea. In fact, the book of ornament is the best gloss on the meaning of the *Autobiography* and on the values to be won by the man-search. For the seed—even its foliation in the sketches of ornament—is only an analogy, and once the analogy is established, Sullivan discusses man and his powers.

These powers, according to Sullivan, are not special gifts. The natural foundation of genius, they are latent in everyone. The ego above all is the "power of initiative," for it is not simply the sum of powers like intellect and sympathy (which are really its agencies) but instinct itself. That it wills to live fully and that this willing is the desire to achieve *its* form explains both Sullivan's notion of functionalism and his reduction of feudalism and democracy to repression and expansive expression. The culture of fear is not a proper soil for life. Speaking of modern man in *Kindergarten Chats*, Sullivan had said that he is "a traitor to himself in suppressing one-half of himself"—that half for which Sullivan himself found fullest expression in his ornament. He speaks of modern man's "prudery and prurience" but also of a stirring he had felt in 1918 (a time of renaissance in the arts), a "new desire, a new, a vaster creative impulse, a new movement of instinct." This movement seemed a harbinger of the democracy he had always championed because it enfranchised the creative: "it is the function of Democracy to liberate, broaden, intensify and focus every human faculty; to utilize every human power now unused, abused, or running to waste."

When the teacher tells this to the student of the *Chats* by way of instructing him in the art of expression, he also tells him that "all geometric forms are at your disposal . . . it is for you to utilize them, to manipulate them, to transmute them, with feeling and intelligence." [6] In *A System of Ornament*, Sullivan demonstrates how this may be done. He begins with a blank block, with the geometrical and rigid, and in a series of essentially mechanical manipulations, he illustrates the artist's control over materials and the first appearance of the imaginative element. In the next series of drawings, the mechanical mode is contrasted with "nature's method of liberating energy"; simple and compound leaf forms undergo their natural, organic, morphological changes, taking on the elaborate forms that Sullivan used as the motifs of other sketches. Organic and mechanical are always contrasted in order to prove, as Emerson said, that there are no straight lines in nature. The will of man makes geometry plastic; "the inorganic and rigid [become] fluent through his powers." If the rigid geometric form is a container of energy, then man by his skill liberates it (Sullivan shows how a pentagon vanishes in a "mobile medium"); and if axes seem rigid, they may be made, when freed from geometry, fluent and responsive to the "most subtle palpitations of life." The heart teaches the head, which now serves it, the lesson of life; feeling bends intellect.

What he had explained in terms of pier, lintel, and arch, he now illustrated with ornament—the supremacy of fluent art. His own ornament was perfectly described in his first paper: "hard lines flow into graceful curves, angularities disappear in a mystical blending of surfaces." [7] But he no longer repudiated this evidence of "exquisite" romanticism, for the feminine was now the instinct which man had denied. Ornament was an example of creation, of the flow of the life-impulse into form. Here one might see the "labile logic of instinct."

For Sullivan, the processes of instinct were always superior to but not separate from those of intellect. He did not believe that art and science were separate activities, any more than feeling and thought or the organic and the inorganic were separate. The fluency of art was "masterful" because it interblended these so-called opposites; art humanized science. He nicely distinguished the dualistic view, the "Euclidian sense of parallel," [8] from the "parallelism" of his own unitary view;

and by "parallelism"—that mystic realm in which art, science, and philosophy fuse—he meant what Emerson had meant by "correspondence." There is, Sullivan said, a "parallelism between man and nature, and between man and his works," for both are contained within the "domain of life, the universal power, or energy which flows everywhere at all times, in all places [the Emersonian Over-Soul which bathes every cove and inlet]. . . ." Man stands within this universe of energy, "a witness, a participant; and, by virtue of his powers a co-creator. . . ." For him the "transcendental logic" of life, of function and form, is a logic of symbolism, of spirit seeking form. Man is a symbol-maker and an interpreter, and thereby makes his world.

The drawings which exemplify this "scientifico-poetic theory" prove that for Sullivan, as for Blake, the release of energy in this ever-creative way was eternal delight. This perhaps is the ultimate lesson of his ornament. It is the play of the artist; it is song, poetry, utterance; and it shows that freedom and spontaneity are not illusions. The fluid symbolism dramatizes the emotions, the rhythms of experience, the flowing of life. Its very plasticity, like its leaf forms, makes it a revelation of the "fullness and the subtle power of life." [9] When it emerges from the surfaces of his building, it declares the values of his vital organic philosophy and beseeches the "form-follows-function mechanists" (as Frederick Gutheim calls those who have misconstrued the genuinely organic) [10] to share the sources of his thought. The ornament reminds one that all forms are symbolic of human feeling and that the creative process the ornament so freely expresses is also the process by which the form of the building may be made to truly fulfill its function. Functions must find an organic, not simply an organized form; and forms, like the ornament itself, must be expressive of more than utilitarian needs. Emerson said that the poet "uses forms according to the life, and not according to the form." [11] And Sullivan, according to John Szarkowski, believed that "man's desire is the most basic

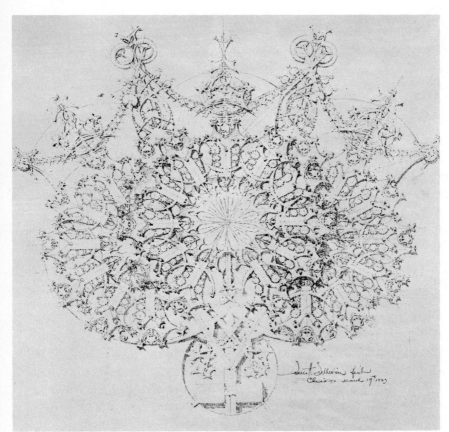

Ornament from *A System of Architectural Ornament*

According with a Philosophy of Man's Powers

of building materials, a . . . framework for his psychic needs the greatest structural problem." [12]

The ornament is a necessary commentary on the building— indeed on the entire organization called culture. It suggests the irrepressible urgings of life and desire and the manifold possibilities of form. It speaks eloquently of an art in which utility is not without beauty, materials not without spirit, the mechanical not without life. It teaches the deepest lesson of *Democratic Vistas,* that materials do not become real, do not satisfy the soul, until they are "touched by emotions, the mind." [13] Here, as in *Leaves of Grass,* is the endless fertility of a man who, having from childhood gone forth everyday, had found himself within the world of nature. The ornament certifies Sullivan's fable of youth.

Perhaps the *Autobiography* was suggested by one of Sullivan's earliest teachers, Taine, who had written of the resemblance between seeds and ideas and of beneficence as the test of art.[14] It is about the idea of beneficent power, about a child's growing awareness of creative impulse and a man's mastery of that impulse for social ends. When it was announced for serial publication, the editor commented on its unusual form: "We doubt very much whether an architect has ever before set out to elucidate a theory or idea . . . by an autobiographical process." [15] There was nothing especially novel in this except the occupation of the writer. Autobiography is a form for growth and education. Wordsworth had used it, and Thoreau and Whitman—and Henry Adams with whose *Education* Whitaker compared Sullivan's book.[16]

Whitaker wrote Sullivan that his work was greater than Adams'. Why he believed this he did not say, though he provided a clue when he wrote elsewhere, "I don't see so much hope as you do." [17] Sullivan's book is his testimony of faith in what he called a stable optimism; a "modern optimisim," he said in *Kindergarten Chats,* ". . . based on a faith in things and assurances fairly well seen. . . . [on] man's powers: and the creative fertility of nature." [18] Though he acknowledged the dark clouds of modern civilization and was no stranger to pessimism, he could not cast his mind in the mold of Adams'. He told Whitaker that he had adopted the third person mode of narration because it permitted him greater freedom.[19] It did, but it also invited comparison with Adams and compelled the contemporary reader for whom Adams had become a spokesman to recognize Sullivan's inversion of Adams' pessimism. Adams, whose brother Brooks spoke of the *Education* as a search for the new mind, considered his education wasted. Sullivan considered his exemplary: the *Autobiography* was an account, more representative and perhaps more usable than Adams', of the education of a new mind.

The theme of the *Autobiography* can be found in all of Sullivan's work. In *Kindergarten Chats,* for example, he says that the "germ" of the solution to the problem of democracy is to be found in the individual man and in his fundamental nature; "having discovered one man, his spirit and his powers, we have discovered all men." In "The Young Man in Architecture," he advocates the normal development of the mind: "if the mind is properly nurtured, properly trained, and left free to act with spontaneity, individuality of expression will come to you as the flower comes to the plant—for it is nature's law." The education of the student in *Kindergarten Chats* partially demonstrates this; and this perhaps explains why Sullivan asked Whitaker to publish the earlier book. He wished to show how an education in the open and relying on common influences, flowered in natural thinking and democratic character. What *Democracy* did for the new sociology, the *Autobiography* does for the new education—imaginatively renders its ideas. When history is driven back to the child, "the unsullied well-spring of power," the man-search is over and the education of democratic man begins.

The pedagogy of course is a part of the new sociology. In "Face to Face" (the chapter title was borrowed from the second section of *Democracy*)[20] Sullivan relates the essential ideas of the earlier book and explicitly formulates his pedagogy. The democratic education he proposes is based on the fact that every child is "the seat of genius." Genius is the "highest form of play with Life's forces" and it must be wisely cultivated by the gardener of the child entrusted to his care. From infancy the child must be permitted to dream and to use his mind in his own way. His identity with things, his mystic sense of closeness to nature, must not be disturbed. Adult feudal thought must not intervene and every sign of feudal fear must be dissolved. He must be allowed to grow in his own "wholesome atmosphere of activities. . . ." The only thing the teacher teaches is the nature of choice.

As the child grows from infancy to childhood, warding, as Sullivan calls this technique, gradually gives way to training or discipline. The child who in the initial stages of growth was watched by Grandfather List now comes under the care of Patrick Sullivan. His powers of body, mind, and heart are coordinated; and the idea of natural powers is suggested to him and shown him objectively. At this time the child, having passed out of his reveries, is excited by the real world and eager for the rudimentary training in the three R's—if only they can be made real to him.

This stage is followed by preadolescence, a time of "vegetative growth" which requires literal instruction. And this is followed by "the Danger Age" of adolescence—no other is more crucial—during which the whole being becomes unstable because of the recrudescence of instinct. The main objective of education at this stage is the fixing of sound character. The kind of education Sullivan has in mind is that which he received from such different teachers as Moses Woolson and Minnie Whittlesey. He wants an "intensive training of the native power to feel straight, to think straight, to act straight. . . ." "To make so clear the moral nature of choice that the individual may visualize the responsibilities involved in the consequences of choice . . . to train the imagination in constructive foresight, in the feeling for real things, in the uses of sentiment, of emotion, in the physical and the spiritual joy of living; to stabilize the gregarious in the social sense; to set forth the dignity of the ego and all egos"—these are some of the aims of an education which would not make growing up absurd. The new powers released in adolescence must be utilized and strengthened by putting on the "heavy work"; but they must also be directed into worthwhile channels. The fruit of democratic education is the worthwhile man, "free in spirit, clean in pride, with footing on the solid earth, with social vision clear and true."

All further education, however technical, must be imbued with this spirit. And all specialities, as Sullivan showed in *Kindergarten Chats,* must be set forth as "Unified social activities." Every discipline—and most urgently that of education—must be understood and utilized as a social function, for man is the moral foundation of civilization. Everything he does is to be tested by whether or not it ministers to "the all-inclusive art of creating out of the cruel feudal chaos of cross purposes, a civilization, in equilibrium, for free men conscious of their powers, and with those powers under moral control." Only such a civilization, Sullivan believed, was worthy of man—and would endure.

If Whitaker had not insisted on the final chapters, the *Autobiography* would have ended with the concluding lines of "Face to Face": *"Thus broadens and deepens to our comprehension the power and the glory of the Democratic Vista!"* The book would have had a simpler unity and would not have been so readily used as literal autobiography. But even though Sullivan yielded to Whitaker's demands (he once informed Sullivan that the architects were impatient with the child and wanted to hear about architecture),[21] he used the additional chapters for his own ends. He applied the moral of his education by contrasting two dreamers and their visions of civilization. He used Daniel Burnham as his personal foil. "Daniel Burnham," he said, "was obsessed by the feudal idea of power. Louis Sullivan was equally obsessed by the beneficent idea of Democratic power." The final chapters develop this opposition of resolute men, and if Burnham seemingly wins it is only because "Daniel chose the easier way, Louis the harder."

Burnham was a man of his time who became eminent because he represented the thought of the multitudes. His heroes were captains of industry, merchant princes, and robber barons; his dream was bigness. According to his biographer, he was a self-made man, "a genuine product of the Middle West, ready to seize opportunity. . . ." [22] Sullivan said that Burnham was the only architect in Chicago who recognized the significance of the movement toward monopolies and trusts; in the tendency toward "bigness, organization, delegation, and intense commercialism, he sensed the reciprocal workings of his own mind." [23] In Sullivan's demonology Burnham is a monopolist; having the passion to sell which Sullivan said was the impelling power in American life, he is also a "colossal merchandiser."

Sullivan acknowledged the power of Burnham's dream but not its beneficence. Even within Burnham's organization he saw its inimical results. He identified with Root, the artist of the firm, who did not always have his way with the merchant and who thereby portended the difficulties of the freelance. The artist was crippled by the merchant's policy—" It is not good policy," Sullivan has Burnham say, "to go much above the general level of intelligence." But then, Sullivan asks, with the possibilities of the World's Fair in mind ("a superb revelation of America's potency—an oration, a portrayal, to arouse that which was hidden, to call it forth into the light"), "of what avail the dream if it be but a dream of misrepresentation?" Why dream at all if the dream "rise not in vision above the general level of intelligence, and prophesy through the medium of clear thinking, true interpretation . . . ?" Burnham, Chief of Construction for the World's Fair, created the White City of his dream.

"That one man's unconscious stupor in bigness, and in the droll phantasy of hero-worship," Sullivan claimed, "did his best and his worst, according to his lights. . . ."

The World's Fair was cursed by more than bigness. It was cursed by eclecticism. Its buildings were "impudently thievish." Except for replicas of Columbus' caravels, there was no evidence that this was a Columbian Exposition celebrating the discovery of America. It celebrated a past not even its own; in spirit and in stone it was a betrayal. Looking back, Sullivan spoke with some justice of the Fair as a cultural virus spreading the feudal contagion. He was thinking not only of the new rash of styles but of the various city plans Burnham had initiated in the aftermath of his success at the Fair and of the World War which had left a new generation wondering, as he did, "whether the discovery of America had proven to be a blessing or a curse to the world of mankind." The World's Fair had provided a test of American culture which, Sullivan believed, American culture had failed.

Veblen would have seen in Burnham's city plan for Chicago a civic setting for conspicuous leisure, and such in fact was Burnham's intention. He admired Haussmann's boulevards and wished to make of Chicago another Paris where the Midwestern idle rich would spend their money. Preempting the lake front for the wealthy, he planned—not a city—but a magnificent pleasure ground; the poor were to benefit not by the city itself but by what the rich spent there. They were planned out, excluded, left to their tenements. Their fate was similar to that of the unemployed who had gathered on the lake front in 1893, and had been driven away by the police so that visitors to the Fair would not see their misery.[24] If Burnham saw as Sullivan had in *Democracy* the mansions on the boulevards and the sweat-shops lining other streets ("not called boulevards because not respectable enough, not well enough paved, not tree-planted and grass-platted, vacant of fair equipages going and coming, and children prettily dressed"), he did not see their economic and civic connections. Beauty, for him, was only a commodity that paid; grandeur was the glory of the city. Burnham had never recognized "the social menace and danger" of the sky-scraper; his organization did not design country banks. Dreaming his feudal dream, he could not imagine, as Sullivan had, "a gorgeous Garden City . . . truly interpreting the aspirations and the heart's desire of the many, every detail carefully considered, every function given its due form, with a sense of humanity at its best, a suffusing atmosphere. . . ."

Planning and building of Burnham's kind, Sullivan believed, added to the precarious instability of modern feudal society. Both were examples of the aggressive will to please oneself and were associated by him with "business is business," a phrase he had reduced in *Democracy* to a single word: "death." This phrase was a euphemism for "survival of the fittest"; it covered the force and fraud of business which Sullivan in turn had uncovered by showing the ways in which business was a man-hunt that could not go on without game. His image for this business society in the *Autobiography* is the stockyards—and it is linked with Burnham's feudal dream when Sullivan mentions Burnham's admiration for his father-in-law, John Sherman, "a big stockyards man."

The stockyards are the underside of Chicago's wealth. In Sullivan's hands the slaughter there becomes a terrifying and sardonic fable of man, his animal farm. Some pigs, he writes, dream of going to Congress; others dream of making the world safe for democracy and when their time comes answer their country's call ("it may be to fill little holes in the ground where poppies grow and bloom"). Those who remain behind, however, serve in their own way: fattened, watered, shipped in "palace" cars, they finally reach the man with the knife; not murdered but "merely slaughtered," they are readied for the table where they are rejoiced in as benefactors of mankind. "Thus may a hog rise," Sullivan comments, "to the heights of altruism. It does not pay to assume lowly origins as finalities, for it is shown that good may come out of the sty, as out of the manger." This is Sullivan's last attempt to awaken men to choice. "What about the other pink and whites at the breast today?" he asks. "Are they to grow up within a culture which shall demand of them their immolation? or shall they not?"

Sullivan probably knew Charles Moore's *Daniel H. Burnham, Architect, Planner of Cities* (1921), that two-volume work of infatuation, just as he knew Mrs. Rensselaer's and Harriet Monroe's finely sympathetic lives of Richardson and Root; and with no prospect of a biographer, he was forced to become his own. He obviously wished to redress the record and to issue his own reprieve from oblivion. But even more—and this measures his stature—he wanted to test the values of his life. The query he put to himself was the perennial one the teacher of *Kindergarten Chats* had spoken of, that question of "advancing age . . . ever intensifying as the years go by and the reckoning-day approaches." The question is almost as old as man: What shall it profit a man if he gain the whole world and lose his own soul? Man is asked to consider the proportion of his life, its "poise, balance, symmetry," and to adjudicate his values. Thus the final chapters, that "Retrospect" of old age, became a moral arena in which the loser in the battle for architecture was crowned with the laurels of spiritual victory. He had chosen the harder way; his search for the meaning of life and of man had a grandeur unknown to the votary of bigness; and above all he had had the courage "to remain steadfast in faith in the presence of such pollution." In that dark time he could still keep faith with the child who, he hoped, would learn through living the organic wisdom he had learned, that "one life surely is enough if lived and fulfilled." On that foundation a new civilization of man might yet be built. The seeds he had garnered were ready and as hope-bearing as those seeds of virtue Thoreau had planted and cared for at Walden Pond. One needed only to remember the powers within the seed-germ and to choose to be a gardener not of "beans for seed," as Thoreau said, but of a "new generation of men." [25]

The essays Sullivan wrote at this time are directly related to and might be said to be the current history of the *Autobiography*. In "The Chicago Tribune Competition," he upheld the second place design of Eliel Saarinen and denounced the jury (who, Whitaker later told him, had not been willing to give a foreigner first prize) for choosing the Gothic design of Raymond Hood.[26] Here, again, were two men, one a master of ideas and the other their slave, who represented for him the opposition between the imaginative and the imaginary, the democratic and the feudal.[27] In another essay published two months later, he supported another master of ideas who had demonstrated, as Sullivan was soon to write in the *Autobiography*, that "clear vision leads to straight thinking, sound thinking to sane action, sane action to beneficent results that shall endure." For Frank Lloyd Wright's Imperial Hotel, having been "thought-built" as Sullivan wrote in his last article on the Tokyo disaster, withstood the earthquake.[28]

The Tokyo disaster for Sullivan was a cataclysm that dramatized all his forebodings and hopes. It was a fateful hour, when the solid masonry buildings—those eclectic buildings the English and the Germans had erected not knowing that they were inviting destruction—"danced their dance of death." In the holocaust he saw a "startling tragedy of ideas, wherein the abstract has crumbled in universal ruin, while one *living* thought and living thing survives"; and this, he claimed, was "the significance of the statement that on the vast stage of the world-drama two ideas, both of them immense in power, confront each other in spectacular appeal to the fears and courage of mankind." Tokyo, now the symbol of civilization, was doomed by "a false premise." But still standing amid the ashes was the Imperial Hotel, and it was not without reason everything Sullivan saw in it: the most significant architectural monument of the modern world. Its architect had vindicated the master, his doctrine of natural thinking and his vision of the future.

Panic and war, dark cloud and storm, earthquake and fire— these were the images of disaster that Sullivan used to heighten his melodramatic vision of the tragedy of ideas. To make alternatives clear and to compel choice, he resorted to a Manichaean dualism of good and evil, light and dark. For the embattled prophet as for the aggressive architect there was something congenial in this simple warfare in which victory was always an inversion. But even more congenial and deeper in his thought were images of natural change, images not of outbreak and revolution but of rhythmic growth, of the seasons of man and nature. His mind, like Henry Adams', was formed by the alterations of summer and winter, country and city. But when freed from the feudal strife of the city, he did not think dualistically or of disaster; he thought, as he tells us in the very chapters that relate his battle for architecture, of the flow of life. Ocean Springs unfolded the lessons of nature that South Reading had first opened to him, and from this vantage he began to realize "the destruction we have wrought." When he returned to the city, he expounded not a naive agrarianism but a philosophy of creation. "Form follows function" formulated that philosophy; the "mobile equilibrium" of civilization described its goal in creation.

The dreamer is known, Sullivan said, by the character of his dream. His dream, momentarily shared and partially fulfilled by a younger generation, was of a new day and new doings, of the modern sunlight that dispelled the moonlit phantoms of shame, of a new art of expression and a new civilization in which individuals were no longer intoxicated with the "luxury of self."

Dreaming when "widest awake," he dreamed of the greatest adventure of man: "the art of developing Democracy into a complete, complex yet simple, working civilization. . . ." [29] To this end he directed the creative good in man and bequeathed the spirit of his work. In the unpublished poem on "The Master," completed within a month of his reception by the Architectural League, he told of his love of the land and its people, how America was his hope and his promise. And then, as Whitman had before him, he foretold how he should pass away yet be nearby because in departing he would give his soul "as a heritage, to animate, to inspire, to urge onward." [30]

APPENDIX

From Louis Sullivan, "Ornamentation of the Auditorium," Industrial Chicago, II (1891), pp. 490-91

"The most notable of the decorations are, of course, to be seen in the main Auditorium. Here the color scheme is broad, simple and grand, consisting of gold and old ivory in graded tones. Three large mural paintings form the pièce de résistance. One of these is placed over the proscenium arch, and one on each of the side walls. Their purpose is to express, allegorically, the two great rhythms of nature, namely, growth and decadence. The central painting consists mainly of figures; the side paintings are outdoor scenes, containing each but a solitary figure, that of the poet communing with nature. The direct expression of these paintings tends toward the musical, for that 'the utterance of life is a song, the symphony of nature,' is the burden of the proscenium composition; in its 'allegro' and 'adagio' are expressed the influence of music. The side paintings are further expressive of the symphony of nature, for in them her tender voice sings joyously or sadly to the attentive soul of the poet, awakening those delicate, responsive harmonies, whose name is inspiration. On one side, corresponding with the allegro of the central painting, is the 'spring song,' a scene at dawn within a wooded meadow, by a gently running stream. The poet is

Proscenium Mural, The Auditorium Building

abroad to greet the lark; the pale tints of sunrise suffuse the
landscape; the early tinge of green is over all; the joy of this
awakening life deeply touches the wandering poet, who sings
in ecstasy, 'O soft melodious springtime, first born of life and
love!'

"The scene then changes to the side corresponding with the
adagio. Here is depicted the natural and calm decline of life.
It is an autumn reverie, the twilight, the symbol of decadence.
The scene is of pathless wilds, in gray, subsiding autumn, where
brown leaves settle through the air, descending one by one to
join the dead, while winds, adagio, breathe shrill funeral lamenta-

Mural, The Auditorium Building

tions. Tired nature here, her task performed, divested of her lovely many-colored garment, withdraws behind a falling veil and sinks to sleep. Sadly musing, the poet turns to descend into the deep and somber valley, conscious that 'a great life has passed into the tomb, and there awaits the requiem of winter's snows.' Thus have all things their rise and decline, their dawn and twilight, their spring song and their autumn reverie, and thus by their symbolism do these mural poems suggest the compensating phases of nature and of human life in all their varied manifestations. Naturally are suggested the light and the grave in music, the joyous and the tragic in drama. The central painting, on its more conventional background of gold, expresses in its many minor figures the manifold influence of music on the human mind—the dance, the serenade, the dirge; while a deeper meaning, conveying the rhythmic significance of life's song, is embodied in special groups and figures wholly symbolical in character. At the right is an altar on which burns the lambent flame of life. Before it poses an exultant figure typifying the dawn of life, the springtime of the race, the early flight of imagination. At the left another altar is seen on which a fire is burning and flickering toward its end; near it the type of twilight, of memory, tenderness and compassion, stands with yearning, outstretched arms. The central group signifies the present, the future, and the past. The present, a lyre in her hand, sits enthroned, the embodiment of song, of the utterance of life. Toward her all the elements of the composition tend, and at this focal point is developed their full significance and power, for the present is the magical moment of life; it is from the present that we take the bearings of the future and of the past."

A BIBLIOGRAPHY
The Writings of Louis Sullivan

1. "Characteristics and Tendencies of American Architecture," *The Inland Architect and Builder*, VI (November, 1885), 58-59. Reprinted in *Kindergarten Chats and Other Writings*, pp. 177-81.

2. "Essay on Inspiration," *The Inland Architect and Builder*, VIII (December, 1886), 61-64. (See Item 14 below.)

3. Reply to "What Are the Present Tendencies of Architectural Design in America?" *The Inland Architect and News Record*, IX (March, 1887), 23-26. Sullivan's extemporaneous remarks on p. 26.

4. "What is the Just Subordination, in Architectural Design, of Details to Mass?" *The Inland Architect and News Record*, IX (April, 1887), 51-54; *Building Budget*, III (April, 1887), 62-63. Partially reprinted in *Kindergarten Chats and Other Writings*, pp. 182-86.

5. "Style," *The Inland Architect and News Record*, XI (May, 1888), 59-60.

6. "The Artistic Use of the Imagination," *The Inland Architect and News Record*, XIV (October, 1889), 38-39.

7. "Ornamentation of the Auditorium," *Industrial Chicago*, Chicago, 1891, Vol. 2, pp. 490-91.

8. "Ornament in Architecture," *Engineering Magazine*, III (August, 1892), 633-44. Reprinted in *Kindergarten Chats and Other Writings*, pp. 187-90.

9. "Emotional Architecture as Compared with Intellectual: A Study in Objective and Subjective," *The Inland Architect and News Record*, XXIV (November, 1894), 32-34. Reprinted in *Kindergarten Chats and Other Writings*, pp. 191-201.

10. "The Tall Office Building Artistically Considered," *Lippincott's*, LVII (March, 1896), 403-409; *The Inland Architect and News Record*, XXVII (May, 1896), 32-34. Reprinted, slightly altered, as "Form and Function Artistically Considered," *The Craftsman*, VIII (July, 1905), 453-58; reprinted in *The Western Architect*, XXXI (January, 1922), 3-11; reprinted in *Kindergarten Chats and Other Writings*, pp. 202-13.

11. "An Unaffected School of Modern Architecture: Will It Come?" *Artist* (New York), XXIV (January, 1899), xxxiii-iv.

12. Unpublished Address to the Chicago Architectural Club, May 1899. Burnham Library.

13. "The Modern Phase of Architecture," *The Inland Architect and News Record*, XXXIII (June, 1899), 40; *The Architectural Annual*, I (1900), 27.

14. "The Master." The third part of "Nature and the Poet," a group of poems beginning with "Inspiration" (1886) and including "Sympathy—a Romanza" (undated). (Dated by Sullivan, July 1, 1899.) Unpublished manuscript in the Burnham Library.

15. Letter in reply to George R. Dean's "Progress before Precedent," *The Brickbuilder*, IX (May, 1900), 96.

16. "The Young Man in Architecture," *The Brickbuilder*, IX (June, 1900), 115-19; *The Inland Architect and News Record*, XXXV (June, 1900), 38-40. Reprinted in *The*

Western Architect, XXXIV (January, 1925), 4-10; *Twice A Year*, No. 2 (Spring-Summer, 1939), 109-21; *Kindergarten Chats and Other Writings*, pp. 214-23.

17. "Remarks at the Second Convention of the Architectural League of America," *The Inland Architect and News Record*, XXXV (June, 1900), 42-43.

18. "Reality in the Architectural Art," *The Interstate Architect and Builder*, II (August 11, 1900), 6-7; *The Inland Architect and News Record*, XXXVI (September, 1900), 16. Reprinted from The Chicago *Tribune*.

19. "Open Letter," *The Interstate Architect and Builder*, II (December 8, 1900), 7.

20. Letter, *The Brickbuilder*, X (June, 1901), 112.

21. "Architectural Style," *The Inland Architect and News Record*, XXXVIII (September, 1901), 16.

22. *Kindergarten Chats.* Serial publication in *The Interstate Architect and Builder*, II-III (February 16, 1901-February 8, 1902). In book form, edited by Claude F. Bragdon (Lawrence, Kansas: Scarab Fraternity Press, 1934); revised version of 1918, *Kindergarten Chats and Other Writings*, edited by Isabella Atley (New York: George Wittenborn, Inc., 1947).

23. "Education," *The Inland Architect and News Record*, XXXIX (June, 1902), 41-42. Reprinted in *Kindergarten Chats and Other Writings*, pp. 224-26.

24. "Natural Thinking: A Study in Democracy." Delivered in part, February 13, 1905. Unpublished manuscript in the Burnham Library.

25. "Reply to Mr. Frederick Stymetz Lamb on 'Modern Use of the Gothic; The Possibility of a New Architectural Style,'" *The Craftsman*, VIII (June, 1905), 336-38.

26. Letter, *The Craftsman*, VIII (July, 1905), 453.

27. "What is Architecture: A Study in the American People of Today," *The American Contractor*, XXVII (January,

1906), 48-54; *The Craftsman*, X (May, June, July, 1906), 145-49, 352-58, 507-13. Reprinted and interpreted by W. G. Purcell, entire issue of *The Northwest Architect*, VIII (October-November, 1943); reprinted in a revised version, *Kindergarten Chats and Other Writings*, pp. 227-41. Printed as *"Was ist Architektur,"* with a foreword by I. K. Pond, by the *Akademie der Künste* (Berlin, January, 1926), in connection with an exhibition, *Ausstellung Neuer Amerikanischer Baukunst.*

28. *Democracy: A Man-Search* (1907-1908). Published on microcards, with an introduction by Hugh Morrison, Louisville Free Public Library (Louisville, 1950); published in book form, with an introduction by Elaine Hedges (Detroit: Wayne State University Press, 1961). Excerpts published in *Twice A Year*, V-VI (Fall-Winter, 1940-Spring-Summer, 1941), 17-28; also "Wherefore the Poet?" *Poetry*, VII (March, 1916), 305-307.

29. "Louis H. Sullivan Emphatically Supports the Viewpoint of Gutzon Borglum Toward American Art," *The Craftsman*, XV (December, 1908), 338.

30. "Is Our Art a Betrayal Rather Than an Expression of American Life?" *The Craftsman*, XV (January, 1909), 402-404.

31. "Suggestions in Artistic Brickwork," foreword to *Artistic Brick*, published by Hydraulic-Press Brick Company (St. Louis, undated [ca. 1910]), pp. 5-13.

32. "Development of Construction," *The Economist* (Chicago), LV (June 24, 1916), 1252; LVI (July 1, 1916), 39-40.

33. *The Autobiography of an Idea*. Serial publication, *Journal of the American Institute of Architects* (June, 1922-September, 1923). Published in book form by the AIA (New York, 1924); by W. W. Norton (New York, 1934); Peter Smith (New York, 1949); Dover (New York, 1956).

34. *A System of Architectural Ornament According with a Philosophy of Man's Powers.* (Plates drawn January 1922-

May 1922). Published by the American Institute of Architects (New York, 1924).

35. "The Chicago Tribune Competition," *The Architectural Record*, LIII (February, 1923), 151-57.

36. "Concerning the Imperial Hotel, Tokyo, Japan," *The Architectural Record*, LIII (April, 1923), 333-52.

37. "Reflections on the Tokyo Disaster," *The Architectural Record*, LV (February, 1924), 113-17. This and the previous essay are reprinted in H. Th. Wijdeveld, *The Life Work of The American Architect, Frank Lloyd Wright,* (Santpoort, Holland, 1925), pp. 101-31.

NOTES

1. Horace Traubel, *With Walt Whitman in Camden* (New York, 1914), III, pp. 25-26.
2. *The Autobiography of an Idea* (New York, 1956; first edition, 1924), p. 274. All unidentified quotations in this chapter are from this source.
3. *The Child: A Study in the Evolution of Man* (London, 1900), p. 464.
4. *The Philosophy of Art* in *Lectures on Art,* translated by John Durand (New York, 1875), I, p. 93.
5. "The Artistic Use of the Imagination," *The Inland Architect and News Record,* XIV (October, 1889), 38-39. The entire address develops Whitman's philosophy; the poem, from the 1860-61 edition, is cited in full.
6. *Louis Sullivan As He Lived: The Shaping of American Architecture* (New York, 1960). Hereafter referred to as Connely.
7. One wonders if he had read Wordsworth's *The Prelude;* see *The Prelude,* VI, 76-94.
8. Sullivan says the move was made in 1869, but Connely corrects him.
9. Here, Sullivan's comment glosses his theory of ornament: "he did not perceive the Euclidian *rigidity,* in the sense that he noted the fluency of Algebra."
10. Woolson's pedagogy, concern for hygiene, passion for botany, and fervor for women's rights, suggest transcendentalist leanings. Sullivan says that he confirmed his love of nature as a source of inspiration.
11. See Winston Weisman, "Philadelphia Functionalism and Sullivan," *Journal of the Society of Architectural Historians,* XX (March, 1961), 3-19.
12. Sigfried Giedion, *Space, Time and Architecture,* third edition (Cambridge, 1959), p. 10.
13. Such characterizations are in fact judgments because Sullivan's belief that

a building bespeaks the personality of the builder is reversible. See Giedion, *Space, Time and Architecture* for a reappraisal of Jenney.

14. Connely, p. 63.

15. Manuscript, Columbia University Library; see Connely, pp. 72-79.

16. "Finished," as Sullivan uses this word elsewhere, denotes the continuous process of culture—"stable motion," the cultural equivalent of his aesthetic ideal of mobile equilibrium, the union of the static and the dynamic in organic or vital form. "Finished" is contrasted with the raw and the decadent.

17. Sullivan obviously learned to read what he called the "physiognomy" of the land. Europe introduced him to the idea of national cultures. The emotional content of his response to England and France is fairly typical and may stand for his actual reaction. The subtle suggestion in the general contrast and in the imagery of wretches-slum and children-garden is the work of the artful writer who was always seeking ways to contrast feudalism and democracy. But for the old man in the Warner Hotel it may be the measure of his own awareness of decline—of what, his friends failing him, might have awaited him. For the imagery might also suggest the "garden city" of his youth and his present condition.

18. See Frank Lloyd Wright, *Genius and the Mobocracy* (New York, 1949). One drawing was dedicated to Edelmann.

19. Connely, pp. 61-63.

20. This may have been the view of the young student; but, summarizing his study of Rome in *Democracy: A Man-Search*, it is more likely the view of the older man.

21. Notebook, manuscript, Columbia University Library. From Taine's work Sullivan might have learned to dramatize history.

22. Taine's *Lectures on Art*, which comprises the books Sullivan read, does not contain such an assertion. Sullivan may have confused what he remembered of Taine with his more recent reading in J. A. Symonds' *The Life of Michelangelo Buonarroti*, a book which undoubtedly colored the account of his experiences in the Sistine Chapel. The question of *momentum*, moreover, was introduced, as we shall see, so that Sullivan might explain it as "the work of a man powerful even in old age.

23. He also admitted: "I was at the school a much shorter time than many others. . . ." This enabled him to maintain that he learned much and speedily but also that everything he stood for had not been learned at the Beaux Arts. Manuscript, Letter, July 25, 1904, Burnham Library; also reprinted with altered punctuation in Claude Bragdon, "Letters from Louis Sullivan," *Architecture*, LXIV (July, 1931), 7-10; and in Bragdon, *More Lives Than One* (New York, 1938), pp. 155-56.

24. Baumann was not, as Sullivan says, a master of one idea. A well-educated German, he played an important and stimulating part in the architectural discussions of the time.

25. The *Autobiography* omits Sullivan's employment with Johnston & Edelmann. (See Connely.) Perhaps Sullivan, always better known for his ornament than for his building, did not wish to weight his achievement on this side. The frescoes of the Moody Tabernacle are excellently described in the Chicago *Times*, May 21, 1876, reprinted in Connely, pp. 83-85.

CHAPTER 2

1. *The Complete Works of Ralph Waldo Emerson*, edited by E. W. Emerson, (Boston and New York, 1903), I, p. 114.
2. *Form and Function*, edited by Harold A. Small (Berkeley and Los Angeles, 1947), pp. 51-57.
3. *Proceedings of the Fourth Annual Convention of the American Institute of Architects* (New York, 1871), pp. 47-54.
4. These addresses are printed in *The Inland Architect and Builder*, VIII (December, 1886), 76-77, 64-65, 61-64.
5. *Ibid.*, 76.
6. Garland, like Sullivan, was indebted to Taine and Whitman. He also preached (if he did not practice long) Veritism, an aesthetic that modified the strictly scientific factual demands of naturalism by insisting that truth is not solely objective fact but fact mediated by individual perception. If naturalism is comparable to the constructional functionalism of the engineer, then realism, balancing the claims of scientific fact and romantic imagination, is comparable to the more organic functionalism Sullivan proposed. It is interesting to note that, like Garland, many of the Chicago architects later abandoned the functional aesthetic; they turned, as he did, to romance—to a romance of styles.
7. "Originality in Design," *The Inland Architect and News Record*, XII (November, 1888), 54.
8. This discussion is from *The Inland Architect* (1885-89). The specific articles are: "The Evolution of an American Style," X (January, 1888), 98; "Development of Architectural Style," XIV (December, 1889), 76-78; "To what extent is it necessary in design to emphasize the essentially structural elements of a building?" IX (May, 1887), 59-62; "Broad Art Criticism," XI (February, 1885), 3-5; "Style," VIII (January, 1887), 99-101; "Characteristics and Tendencies of American Architecture," VI (November, 1885), 58-59.
9. Ray Ginger, *Altgeld's America: The Lincoln Ideal* VERSUS *Changing Realities* (New York, 1958), first places Sullivan in the social context of his time; Vincent Scully, Jr., "Louis Sullivan's Architectural Ornament, a Brief Note Concerning Humanist Design in the Age of Force," *Perspecta, The Yale Architecture Journal*, 5, 1959, pp. 73-80, first fully realizes the humanistic intent of Sullivan's architectural work. Scully

says: "For Sullivan . . . buildings were not so much ambients within which human beings might move—which has always been the Wrightian tradition—as sculptural presences which might complement and challenge human beings and, through physical association, awaken in the new mass age a renewed sense of the possible dignity of an active human presence in the world."

Had he lived, John Wellborn Root might have shared this role with Sullivan. Intuitive and sensitive, a Swedenborgian with romantic feelings for nature, he believed that materialism is a mode of spirit. He was fully aware of the architect's responsibility to the community. In his excellent writings, one is disturbed only by his analogies, which are drawn from the fashionable world of the gentleman, and by his easy belief in commerce as the stable, conserving, and beneficent force of modern civilization.

10. See *Kindergarten Chats*, Chapter XXIX.
11. See *Kindergarten Chats*, Chapter XXV: "You must have also a pretty clear idea what it is that you feel. . . ."
12. *The Journals of Ralph Waldo Emerson*, edited by E. W. Emerson and W. E. Forbes (Boston, 1909-14), IV, pp. 108-10.
13. The above quotations are from "Characteristics and Tendencies of American Architecture," *The Inland Architect and Builder*, VI (November, 1885), 58-59.
14. *Kindergarten Chats and Other Writings* (New York, 1947), pp. 29-30.
15. *The Autobiography of an Idea* (New York, 1956), pp. 301-303. In Sullivan's day, architects were not embarrassed by poetry, but a forty-five minute rhapsody might have been too much. McLean printed the entire essay, which Sullivan introduced by remarking: ". . . to write an essay on inspiration is something like writing an essay on the eyesight: it is something that we all know about but it is very difficult to define. Therefore I will indulge in no definitions, but instead of dealing in plain language, I will treat my subject in the language of metaphor." The essay, from which the following quotations are taken, is printed in *The Inland Architect and Builder*, VIII (December, 1886), 61-64; The introductory remarks from *Ibid.*, p. 79.
16. "Song of Myself," §3.
17. Sullivan described the murals in detail, elaborating the meaning of "Inspiration" and allying it with music, in "Ornamentation of the Auditorium," *Industrial Chicago* (Chicago, 1891), II, pp. 490-91.
18. "What are the present tendencies of architectural design in America?" *The Inland Architect and News Record*, IX (March, 1887), 23-26.
19. Taine, *The Philosophy of Art* in *Lectures on Art*, translated by John Durand (New York, 1875), I, pp. 73-75.
20. See *The Autobiography of an Idea*, pp. 299 ff.
21. "What is the just subordination, in architectural design, of details to

mass?" *The Inland Architect and News Record*, IX (April, 1887), 51-54. See also, Sullivan, "Ornament in Architecture," *Engineering Magazine*, III (August, 1892), 633-44, where he develops the early idea in terms of what he learned from Whitman and in the light of his own practice.

22. He noted that this is not the case with great artists: ". . . their art in all its potentiality is born with them, and prophesies in earliest childhood the destiny of its great consummation." Here is a thesis of the *Autobiography*.

23. "Style," *The Inland Architect and News Record*, XI (May, 1888), 59-60.

24. "The Artistic Use of the Imagination," *The Inland Architect and News Record*, XIV (October, 1889), 38-39.

25. "Ornament in Architecture," *Engineering Magazine*, III (August, 1892), 633-44.

26. "The Tall Office Building Artistically Considered," *Lippincott's*, LVII (March, 1896), pp. 403-409. Vincent Scully, Jr., *Modern Architecture: The Architecture of Democracy* (New York, 1961), p. 19, says that Sullivan "brought into the mass metropolis—in terms of its new program of skyscraper office building—a dignified image of human potency and force."

27. Cited by Montgomery Schuyler, "Last Words About the Fair," *The Architectural Record*, III (January-March, 1894), 292. For a good sampling of opinion on the Fair, see William A. Coles and Henry Hope Reed, Jr., *Architecture in America: A Battle of Styles* (New York, 1961).

28. "Pappa, what kind is the architecture?" he rapturously asked [at Grant's tomb].
    "Classic architecture!"
    "Is classic architecture the finest, Pappa?"
    "I feel, since the Greeks and the Romans, who were after all the most advanced of mankind, used it," said Pappa, "it *is* the finest!"
    Paul Rosenfeld, *The Boy in the Sun* (New York, 1928), p. 31.

29. *The Inland Architect and Builder*, VIII (December, 1886), 90.

30. "Architecture at the World's Columbian Exposition," *The Century Magazine*, XLIV (May, 1892), 89.

31. *The Theory of the Leisure Class* (New York, 1934), p. 198. Originally published in 1899.

32. *Modern Building: Its Nature, Problems, and Forms* (New York, 1937), p. 123.

CHAPTER 3

1. "The firm of Gage Bros. & Co . . . offered to pay additional rent . . . on the increased cost of employing Mr Sullivan and erecting such a front as he should design. They did so because they thought it would benefit their business in an equal degree. They put an exact commercial value on Mr. Sullivan's art, otherwise he would not have been called in." *The Brickbuilder*, VIII (December, 1899), 254.

2. "Influence of Steel Construction and of Plate Glass upon the Development of Modern Style," *The Inland Architect and News Record,* XXVIII (November, 1896), 34-36.

   Though Sullivan was unwilling to resume partnership with Adler, he was not ungenerous. When Adler died in 1900, Sullivan designed the border of his memorial portrait. See *The Inland Architect,* XXV (May, 1900).

3. "Chicago," *The Inland Architect and News Record,* XLV (June, 1905), 47.

4. *The Inland Architect and News Record,* XXXIII (June, 1899), 37; LII (October, 1908), 44.

5. *The Inland Architect and News Record,* XXXIII (June, 1899), 40. The convention was also reported in *The Brickbuilder,* which closely followed the activities of the League in the next few years, and in *The Architectural Annual,* I (1900), the "official" publication of the League. F. L. Wright attended.

6. "Architectural League of America," *The Brickbuilder,* VIII (June, 1899), 111, *The Inland Architect and News Record,* XXXV (June, 1900), 42.

7. *The Brickbuilder,* IX (May, 1900) 91-92. Sullivan's reply is on p. 96.

8. *The Inland Architect and News Record,* XXXV (June, 1900), 42. Sullivan's remarks follow, pp. 42-43.

9. "Architectural Education," *The Brickbuilder,* IX (June, 1900), 123.

10. "The Architect," *The Brickbuilder,* IX (June, 1900), 127; *The Inland Architect and News Record,* XXXV (June, 1900), 43. For an account of the reception of Sullivan's keynote speech, see *The Interstate Architect & Builder,* II (June 16, 1900), 1.

11. *The Interstate Architect & Builder,* II (June 23, 1900) 1; (August 11, 1900), 1; (December 22, 1900), 11-20.

12. *The Interstate Architect & Builder,* II (December 8, 1900), 7, 8-9. Characteristically, Sullivan defended his ornamental designs; he did not seem to mind the skyscrapers of this period that borrowed his solution.

13. *The Inland Architect and News Record,* XXXIII (June, 1899), 43.

14. A. W. Barker, "Louis H. Sullivan, Thinker and Architect," *The Architectural Annual,* II (1901), 49-66, reviewed Sullivan's career and mentioned the *Chats.* It is evident that Sullivan supplied the material. *The Architectural Annual* (p. 284) also described *The Interstate Architect* in order to extol the *Chats.* Much of the issue was devoted to Sullivan: his portrait served as a frontispiece, and two articles and a pictorial section (noteworthy for several sketches of ornament) covered his achievement. Part of "Criticism" from the *Chats* was quoted (pp. 19-20) and Sullivan's sayings interlarded the editorial pages. See also "Appendix A," *Kindergarten Chats and Other Writings* (New York, 1947), pp. 243-45.

15. *Kindergarten Chats,* edited by Claude F. Bragdon (Lawrence, Kansas, 1934), p. vi.

16. *The Brickbuilder,* X (June, 1901), 112.

17. "L'Art Nouveau and American Architecture," *The Brickbuilder,* XII (October, 1903), 205.

18. In "What is Architecture" (1906), Sullivan criticized the aimlessness of architectural periodicals. These periodicals were reviewed in *The Architectural Annual,* II (1901), 281-84. Of *The Inland Architect,* it said: ". . . it fails to represent the aspirations or even the best efforts of the profession in the Middle West . . . as a whole its make-up is lacking in purpose. . . ." McLean later took over *The Western Architect.*

19. "Is Architecture a Living Art?" *The Inland Architect and News Record,* XXIX (April, 1897), 25-26; (February, 1897), 4-7; XXXIII (July, 1899), 46.

20. *The Inland Architect and News Record,* XXIV (November, 1894), 32-34. Unless noted, the following quotations are from this source.

21. *The Journals of Ralph Waldo Emerson,* III, p. 276.

22. *Young Emerson Speaks,* edited by Arthur C. McGiffert, Jr. (Boston, 1938), p. 52.

23. *Observations on the Growth of the Mind* (Boston, 1829), p. 31.

24. Personified in this address, expression is feminine. Sullivan revealed a general attitude of the time when he spoke of her as "the perfection of the physical . . . and the uttermost attainment of emotionality." In this instance he anticipated the "feminine" ornament of the Schlesinger & Mayer Department Store. He had not forgotten the masculine eloquence of the Wainwright and the Guaranty Buildings; rather, it seems, he had become aware of the androgynous character of the artist. His theory of ornamentation is not explained adequately here. Instead his own personal need is revealed: "In her companionship, imaginative thought, long searching, has found its own, and lives anew, immortal, filled with sensibility, graciousness and the warm blood of a fully rounded maturity." The best account of the ways in which Sullivan's ornament enacts the drama of forces and gives live and movement to his buildings is Vincent Scully, Jr., "Louis Sullivan's Architectural Ornament, a Brief Note Concerning Humanist Design in the Age of Force," *Perspecta, The Yale Architectural Journal,* 5, 1959, pp. 73-80.

25. *Lippincott's,* LVII (March, 1896), 403-409. Unless noted, the following quotations are from this source.

26. *Leaves of Grass,* 1855 Preface.

27. *The Brickbuilder,* IX (June, 1900), 115-19. The quotations in the previous paragraph and those that follow are from this source.

28. By this time, Sullivan was aware of John Dewey. In "Reality in the Architectural Art," an editorial reprinted from the Chicago *Tribune* in *The Inland Architect and News Record,* XXXVI (September, 1900), 16, he speaks of the new education and its "science of thinking." The aim of

this education is to help the mind acquire a sense of "reality"—of real things, not of abstractions.

29. "Literary Ethics," *The Complete Works of Ralph Waldo Emerson*, I, p. 186.

30. Almost all quotations are from the most recent and most available edition, *Kindergarten Chats and Other Writings* (New York, 1947). This edition incorporates Sullivan's revisions. The serial publication in *The Interstate Architect & Builder* (1901-1902) and the partially revised edition by Claude F. Bragdon (Lawrence, Kansas, 1934) have also been used to insure fidelity to the development of Sullivan's thought.

31. "Song of Myself," § 2.

32. Paul Goodman, "A Study of Modern Design," *Arts*, XXXV (January, 1961), 21, compares the *Vorkurs* of the Bauhaus, invented by Johannes Itten, with Sullivan's educational program in *Kindergarten Chats*. Both, he says, are applications of psychologically oriented progressive education, and their aim is "to break down the barrier between the organism and the environment in order that the student's action and work may become continuous with his way-of-being-in-the-world." This education, in Itten's words, repudiates "the old dualistic world-concept which envisaged the ego in opposition to the universe. . . ." For Goodman such an educational program is not to be associated with mysticism; he calls it "the true science of man." For Sullivan's attack on dualism, see Chapter IV.

33. *Leaves of Grass*, 1855 Preface.

34. Pointing out the moral content of the phrase, form follows function, Paul Goodman notes that "it was a revolt against hypocrisy and concealment, full in the line of Ibsen and Walt Whitman, and contemporary with *The Theory of the Leisure Class.*" "A Study in Modern Design," p. 21.

35. *Thus Spake Zarathustra*, III, Chapter XLIX.

36. *The Complete Works of Ralph Waldo Emerson*, I, p. 63.

37. *Ibid.*, p. 64.

38. The student tries to write a poem about a butterfly—about Psyche. This, like his attempt to write about a weed, was suggested by Whitman. One of the drawings in *Leaves of Grass* (1860-61 edition) is of a butterfly on the poet's finger.

39. "Appendix A," *Kindergarten Chats and Other Writings*, p. 244.

40. "Appendix C," *Kindergarten Chats and Other Writings*, p. 248. Sullivan answered Peabody in the *Chats*: "If his conception of the creative impulse is on a par with his scholarship I smile and shudder with him." He brought the *Chats* to a close with a chapter on the creative impulse (Chapter L) and in the original installment wrote: "I do not shudder lest God come nigh: one must be a 'scholar' and a president of the American Institute of Architects to do that." Sullivan attacks the genteel guardians of culture throughout the *Chats,* but most directly in "On Scholarship" (Chapter XL).

CHAPTER 4

1. "Reply to Mr. Frederick Stymetz Lamb on 'Modern Use of the Gothic; The Possibilities of a New Architectural Style,' " *The Craftsman,* VIII (June, 1905), 338.

2. *Democratic Vistas* in *Leaves of Grass and Selected Prose,* edited by Sculley Bradley (New York, 1949), p. 513.

3. Lamb, "The Modern Use of the Gothic; The Possibilities of a New Architectural Style," *The Craftsman,* VIII (May, 1905), 150-70; Hamlin, "Style in Architecture," *The Craftsman,* VIII (June, 1905), 331.

4. "Louis H. Sullivan Emphatically Supports the Viewpoint of Gutzon Borglum Toward American Art," *The Craftsman,* XV (December, 1908), 338.

5. "Reply to Mr. Frederick Stymetz Lamb . . .," *The Craftsman,* VIII (June, 1905), 336-38.

6. "What is Architecture: A Study in the American People of Today," *American Contractor,* XXVII (January, 1906), 48-54; reprinted in *The Craftsman,* X (May, June, July, 1906), 145-49, 352-58, 507-13.

7. Connely, p. 221.

8. One of the key words of Sullivan's time was "reality." It was associated with the honesty of science, but it was not opposed to idealism. Sullivan's generation wished to detach idealism from what Van Wyck Brooks called "the malady of the ideal" and to attach it to "real" things.

9. For all that follows on Sullivan's reading, see the auction catalogue and the list of books at Ocean Springs in the Sullivan collection of the Burnham Library. Most of the books at Ocean Springs, with the exception of a few books of the order of Hawthorne's novels and Arnold's *The Light of Asia,* are either light, popular literature or serious treatises on agriculture, botany, and the cultivation of roses.

10. Ralph Barton Perry, *The Present Conflict of Ideals* (New York, 1918), p. 39.

11. A. A. Roback, *History of American Psychology* (New York, 1952), pp. 133-34.

12. "The New Psychology," *Andover Review,* II (1884), 285; "Review of G. Tarde's *Psychologie économique,*" *Journal of Political Economy,* (December, 1902), cited by Joseph Dorfman, *Thorstein Veblen and His America* (New York, 1934), p. 210; *Psychology* (New York, 1887), p. 245; "The New Psychology," p. 288.

13. The Contemporary Science Series, edited by Havelock Ellis, (London, 1900).

14. (New York and London, 1904), 2 vols.

15. (New York, 1890), 2 vols.

16. Subtitled *An Economic Study of the Evolution of Institutions* (New York, 1899).

17. These quotations and those that follow are from Lloyd, *Man, The Social Creator* (New York, 1906) and Triggs, *The Changing Order: A Study of Democracy* (Chicago, 1905).

18. *The Inland Architect and News Record,* XXXIX (June, 1902), 41.

19. *Social Thought in America: The Revolt Against Formalism* (New York, 1949).

20. Manuscript, Burnham Library.

21. XLV (March, 1905), 20.

22. This and the previous quotation from Emerson are 'from *Nature, The Complete Works of Ralph Waldo Emerson,* I, pp. 10, 59.

23. *Ibid.,* pp. 8, 18.

24. *Ibid.,* 10.

25. "Song of Myself," § 5.

26. Cited by Ginger, *Altgeld's America,* p. 90.

27. *The Education of Henry Adams* (New York, 1931 [1918]), pp. 340 ff.

28. *Autobiography,* p. 232.

29. It was completed April 18, 1908; it was published on microcards by the Louisville Free Public Library, with an introduction by Hugh Morrison (Louisville, 1950), and in book form, edited and introduced by Elaine Hedges (Detroit, 1961). The references are to the last edition.

30. *Louis Sullivan: Prophet of Modern Architecture* (New York, 1935), p. 237.

31. This melodrama has many antecedents in American thought; in fact, Sullivan, sometimes using the older language of religion and more often the newer language of modern thought, supplies a new version of what Charles L. Sanford calls the quest for paradise. See Sanford, *The Quest For Paradise: Europe and the American Moral Imagination* (Urbana, 1961).

32. ".The Young Man in Architecture," *The Inland Architect and News Record,* XXXV (June, 1900), 38.

33. *Democratic Vistas,* p. 500.

34. *The Complete Works of Ralph Waldo Emerson,* I, p. 162.

CHAPTER 5

1. Connely, p. 274.

2. *The Riddle of the Universe,* trans. by Joseph McCabe (New York and London, 1900), p. 147.

3. *The Economist* (Chicago), LV (June 24, 1916), 1252; LVI (July 1, 1916), 39-40. Here, perhaps, is the first retrospective glance and the ground work of the last chapters of the *Autobiography.*

4. Manuscript, Letter of Whitaker to Sullivan, December 3, 1923, Burnham Library.

5. The plates were drawn from January 1922 to May 1922; the book was

published by the American Institute of Architects (New York, 1924). Unidentified quotations in the discussion that follows are from this source.

6. *Kindergarten Chats and Other Writings*, pp. 163-68.
7. "Characteristics and Tendencies of American Architecture," *The Inland Architect and Builder*, VI (November, 1885), 58.
8. He took this distinction from Claude Bragdon, *Architecture and Democracy* (New York, 1918), pp. 52-55.
9. "What is Architecture . . .," *The American Contractor*, XXVII (January, 1906), 53.
10. *Frank Lloyd Wright on Architecture* (New York, 1941), p. xviii.
11. *The Complete Works of Ralph Waldo Emerson*, III, p. 21.
12. *The Idea of Louis Sullivan* (Minneapolis, 1956), p. 26.
13. P. 526.
14. *Lectures on Art*, I, pp. 99, 266.
15. *Journal of the American Institute of Architects*, X (March, 1922), 75.
16. Manuscript, Letter of Whitaker to Sullivan, September 26, 1923, Burnham Library.
17. Manuscript, Letter of Whitaker to Sullivan, June 15, 1923, Burnham Library.
18. *Kindergarten Chats and Other Writings*, p. 169. By speaking of "acceleration" on the previous page, Sullivan showed his familiarity with Adams' *Education*, which appeared in time for him to use it in the last chapters of the revision of the *Chats*.
19. Manuscript, Letter of Sullivan to Whitaker, January 28, 1922, Burnham Library.
20. The *Autobiography* is the source of the following discussion. "Face to Face" also refers to I *Corinthians* 13: "When I was a child, I spake as a child, I understood as a child, I thought as a child; but when I became a man, I put away childish things.
    For now we see through a glass darkly; but then face to face. . . ."
21. Manuscript, Letter of Whitaker to Sullivan, September 22, 1922, Burnham Library.
22. Charles Moore, *Daniel H. Burnham, Architect, Planner of Cities* (Boston and New York, 1921), I, p. 117.
23. See Burnham's article on how to set up an architectural office composed of specialists in *The Inland Architect and News Record*, XXXV (June, 1900), 75-76.
24. Ginger, *Altgeld's America*, p. 249.
25. "The Beanfield," *Walden*.
26. *The Architectural Record*, LIII (February, 1923), 151-57; Manuscript, Letter of Whitaker to Sullivan, February 21, 1923, Burnham Library.
27. The distinctions between the imaginative and the imaginary were taken again from Bragdon, *Architecture and Democracy*, p. 52.

28. "Concerning the Imperial Hotel, Tokyo, Japan," *The Architectural Record*, LIII (April, 1923), 333-52; "Reflections on the Tokyo Disaster," *The Architectural Record*, LV (February, 1924), 113-17. All the articles in *The Architectural Record* restate Sullivan's philosophy briefly and clearly.

29. *Kindergarten Chats and Other Writings*, p. 163. Sullivan knew that his dream was not new; what was new, he believed, was the fact that in the modern world men at last clearly saw it. That it was a man's dream and a dream of man and was acknowledged made it realizable. Thoreau bespoke Sulllivan's belief when he wrote in *Walden:* "The poet or the artist never yet had so fair and noble a design but some of his posterity at least could accomplish it."

30. *Nature and the Poet*, Manuscript, Burnham Library.

 INDEX

James, William, ix, 89, 99, 109, 110, 126
  The Principles of Psychology, 96, 102
Jastrow, Joseph, 98
Jenney, Major William Le Baron, 17
  Home Insurance Company Building, 32
Jevons, William Stanley, 18
Johns Hopkins University, 102
Johnston, Joseph, 22
Johnston & Edelmann, 23

K

Kidd, Benjamin, *Principles of Western Civilization*, 97
Kindergarten Chats (Sullivan), 13, 14, 36, 37, 39, 40, 45, 51, 57, 69, 70-81, 108, 114, 122, 124, 125, 128, 132, 133, 135, 139
  method of, 20
  mode of instruction in, 18
  neglect of, 58, 80
  origins of, 57
  structure of, 10

L

Lamb, Frederick Stymetz, 86
Lanier, Sidney, *The Science of English Verse*, 95
"Last Judgment, The" (Michelangelo), 20
Law of Psychic Phenomena, The (Hudson), 99
Lawrence, D. H., 101
Lawson, Thomas, *Frenzied Finance*, 95
Lavater, Johann Kaspar, *Essays on Physiognomy*, 99
Leaves of Grass (Whitman), 1, 132
Lewis and Clark Expedition, 94

Life and Religion (Müller), 94
Lincoln, Abraham, 107
List, Andrienne: (see Sullivan, Mrs. Andrienne List)
List, Anna Mattheus, 6, 14
List, Henri, 6, 7, 11-12, 13, 14, 102, 134
Loeb, Jacques, 98
Lloyd, Henry D., 32, 104, 114
  Man, The Social Creator, 96, 105, 107-108
London, 19
Lotos Club, 17, 18, 22
Lowell, James Russell, 79
Lübke, Wilhelm, *History of Architecture*, 30

M

McKim, Charles, 59
McLean, R. C., 28, 53, 54
  on "Essay on Inspiration," 36
McMaster, John Bach, *A History of the People of the United States*, 95
Maine Woods, The (Thoreau), 13
Man, The Social Creator (Lloyd), 96, 105, 107-108
Marshall Field Wholesale Store (Richardson), 35
Masonic Temple, Boston, 10
Massachusetts Institute of Technology, 14, 15
"Master, The" (Sullivan), 142
Mazzini, Giuseppe, 108
Mead, George Herbert, 98
Melville, Herman, 19, 32, 114
Michelangelo, 3, 22, 126-127
  "The Last Judgment," 20
Millet, Jean François, 107
"Modern Phase of Architecture, The" (Sullivan), 55
Monroe, Harriet, 139

THE GERM: THE SEAT OF POWER

Above is drawn a diagram of a typical seed with two cotyledons. The cotyledons are specialized rudimentary leaves containing a supply of nourishment sufficient for the initial stage of the development of the germ.

The Germ is the real thing; the seat of identity. Within its delicate mechanism lies the will to power: the function which is to seek and eventually to find its full expression in form.

The seat of power and the will to live constitute the simple working idea upon which all that follows is based—as to efflorescence.

A System of Architectural Ornament According with a Philosophy of Man's Powers.
Louis Sullivan